DISCARD
WITHDRAWAL

The Year My Parents
Ruined My Life

The Year My Parents Ruined My Life

MARTHA FREEMAN

Holiday House/New York

Library of Congress Cataloging-in-Publication Data
Freeman, Martha, 1956—
The year my parents ruined my life / by Martha Freeman. — 1st ed.
p.   cm.
Summary: Twelve-year-old Kate has her entire world turned upside-
down when she has to move from California to snowy Pennsylvania,
where she tries to adjust to a new climate, a new school, and
new friends.
ISBN 0-8234-1324-1
[1. Moving, Household—Fiction.   2. Pennsylvania—Fiction.]
I. Title.
PZ7.F87496Ye   1997   97-19395   CIP   AC
[Fic]—dc21

For old friends in California
and new friends in Pennsylvania

The Year My Parents
Ruined My Life

Chapter One

Saturday, October 4, Belletoona, Pennsylvania: Cloudy with a chance of showers.

Kate Sommers had been kidnapped.

Yesterday she was hustled onto a plane against her will and flown practically across the entire country. She was forced to stay the night in an ugly motel and eat greasy scrambled eggs for breakfast. Now she was strapped into the backseat of a big car driven by a paunchy man in a dark suit.

And where were her parents? Her parents, who were supposed to love her and protect her?

That was the worst part.

It was her parents who had kidnapped her.

"Snow? Oh sure, we get some. Wish it was more," Mr. Douglas, the man in the dark suit, was saying to Kate's dad. "I love the white stuff. Can't get enough."

As he spoke, Mr. Douglas pulled his car into the driveway of another house that looked like a two-story shoe box. He was a real estate agent. This was the sixth house they had seen that morning, and Kate didn't need to leave the backseat to know what this one looked like inside: flowered wallpaper, brick fireplace, family room in the basement.

"Come on, girls," said Kate's dad. "This could be the one!"

Kate buttoned the collar of her jacket and stayed put. Danielle, her six-year-old sister, flung herself out of the car, shouting, "I want to see *my* room! I want to see *my* room!"

The little kiss-up, Kate thought.

Mr. Douglas opened the front door, and Kate's dad and sister disappeared inside. Mom, still in the driveway, signaled for Kate to roll down the window. "Sitting this one out?" she asked.

"I will never look at another house as—" Kate began.

"Okay, okay." Mom had been listening to Kate gripe all morning. "Let me tell you something, honey. I'm a California girl, same as you. Until we pulled out the map, I thought Pennsylvania was someplace around Maine. I've got a job I like, then there's my mother, my friends . . ."

Her voice trailed off. "But this is important to your dad," she finally said, "and it's only fair that we —"

"Angela!" Dad's head popped out of an upstairs window. "Come on in, sweetheart! You've got to see this *fantastic* laundry room!"

Mom looked at the sky as if silently counting to ten. Then she squared her shoulders and looked back at Kate. "I am going to make the best of things," she said. "And so are you. Now, excuse me while I look at a *fantastic* laundry room."

Kate shook her head. What had gotten into her parents? Why were they determined to ruin her life? Sure, she knew her dad was always talking about his happy childhood in the East. She knew his company had closed its lawn mower factory in southern California and offered him a better job managing a snow shovel factory here. Still, who in their right mind would trade a sunny beach for this cold, gray, rain-soaked place?

Back at the motel that afternoon, Danielle read a magazine she had found on the TV set, *Pennsylvania Today.* Dad and Mom shuffled photos of the houses they'd looked at. Kate was channel surfing and stopped at a local weather report. Yesterday had been a perfect beach day at home in Isla Nada — before she was kidnapped.

". . . unseasonably cold the rest of the week," said the weatherman. He was wearing a red-and-green-plaid jacket, like he was ready for Christmas. "The long-range weather models show a pattern that could give us snow by Thanksgiving." Kate didn't see why he sounded so cheerful about it.

Kate's dad pointed to one of the photos. "I think we have a winner," he said. "Do you agree, Angela?"

"It's a darling house, Coldwell. But are you sure about that furnace? I thought those old furnaces—"

"Same as we had when I was a boy. Never gave us a moment's trouble," Dad said.

"Well, if you're sure . . ." Kate's mom didn't sound a bit sure, and Kate could almost see her thinking: *Make the best of things.* "If you're sure, then so am I," Mom said firmly. "Let's make an offer."

Kate had no intention of moving to Belletoona, Pennsylvania. She didn't know how she was going to get out of it, but if she and her best friend, Molly, put their heads together, they'd come up with some kind of scheme. They always did, right?

While Dad was talking to Mr. Douglas on the phone, Kate picked up a picture of the house. This one was different from the others—old, made of stone, small bedrooms. The dining room had this disgusting pink polka-dot wallpaper. There was no family room in the basement either, just the furnace that worried her mom, and a lot of cobwebby pipes.

"This one's yours." Mom pointed to an upstairs window.

"The guest room, you mean," said Kate.

Mom's look was like a yellow caution light. "Kate, I've been as patient as I know how to be," she said. "But this little game has got to end."

Danielle looked up from her magazine when she sensed Kate might be in trouble. "Did you know Pennsylvania produces more chocolate than any other state?" she asked. "I *want* to move to Belletoona, Mother. I'm going to make new friends and go to a brand-new school."

Kate wondered how bad the punishment was for strangling a total pest. "Aren't we the little angel?" she snarled.

"Kate Sommers," said Mom, and now the light flashed red. "That is *enough*. I know it's hard to move at your age. But the family is moving. End of discussion."

Mom was being totally unreasonable. No point arguing now. So Kate fumed while Mom explained things for the zillionth time: This had been a scouting mission so that the girls could see the town. The family would fly back to California tomorrow, and in two weeks—only two weeks—Dad would start work here in Pennsylvania.

"You and I and Danielle will stay longer in California to pack up and say good-bye," Mom went on. "If the house sells, we'll be back here before Christmas."

Kate couldn't help it. "What have I done to deserve this?" she wailed. "It's so unfair!"

Mom didn't say anything for a minute, just looked out the window at the rain. When she spoke, she seemed to be talking to herself. "Don't think of it as unfair. Think of it as character-building."

My character's built already, Kate thought. In Isla Nada, California, I'm president of the sixth-grade class, girlfriend of an awesomely gorgeous thirteen-year-old surfer, best friend of Molly Blossom, the class secretary.

In Belletoona, Pennsylvania, who am I? Nobody.

Kate was a planner. She already had the rest of her sixth-grade year figured out: Josh was going to take her to the Valentine's dance, just like she planned. She was going to play volleyball for the Isla Nada Stingrays this spring, just like she planned. And she was going to learn to skate vert next summer, just like she planned.

If her family really moved, she would miss them—even the total pest. But for Kate Sommers, life anyplace other than Isla Nada, California, was unthinkable.

Chapter Two

Wednesday, November 26, Isla Nada, California: Night and early morning low clouds burning off by midday. Highs in the mid to upper 70s.

"Don't cry, Kate. Or I'll start up again. Anyway, they do have phones in . . . oh, golly, I forgot what it's called again. Something fishy, right?" Molly's voice on the phone sounded far away, and Kate was only at her gramma's—not even twenty minutes from her old house. The moving van had taken everything away Monday. Mom, Danielle, and Kate had come here so that they'd have beds to sleep in their last two nights in California. At three o'clock today, they were getting on the plane.

"Belletoona, like I haven't told you a zillion times," Kate said. "You gotta learn to spell it so you can write me. Gramma stuck stationery in my suitcase this morning. Promise you'll write back."

"Of course I will, *chica*. You'd be my best friend even if you lived at the North Pole. . . . Oh, golly, now you're crying again."

Kate couldn't help it. She had tried everything— threats, promises, tantrums. When the real estate lady put the For Sale sign on their house in Isla Nada, Kate painstakingly stenciled SOLD on poster board and tacked it on top. Daddy laughed. But the next morning the Sold sign went out with the trash. Then Molly had the idea Kate should try starving herself. She skipped breakfast and got all faint and pale, but Mom brought tacos and french fries to school at lunch, so, of course, she had to eat.

Desperate, Kate tried to bring Gramma into it. "Think how lonely she'll be without us!" she said to her mom, when what she really meant was: Think how lonely we'll be without her!

But Gramma—that traitor—sided with the grown-ups, insisting she would be fine. What did Kate think, she was one of those helpless widows with nothing but a poodle? Didn't she swim in the ocean every morning? Wasn't she president of her tennis club this year? And she promised to visit once the weather got warm. July maybe.

A month ago, another family had bought Kate's house. After that, Kate, Danielle, and their mom lived in a maze of packing boxes. Monday, after the moving van left, Kate walked through her house saying good-bye. With the furniture gone, the rooms looked dinky and sad, especially the pale, ghostly places where pictures and posters used to be. It was like looking at a face, only the eyes, the nose and the mouth were gone so you couldn't tell whose face it was anymore.

That's me in Pennsylvania, Kate thought. Nobody will know I'm me.

"You there, *chica?*" Molly sounded worried. "It's not like you're *really* becoming a nun. Come on, remember Operation Defrost!"

Operation Defrost. She and Molly had come up with it after everything else had failed. Kate had to go to Belletoona, but only long enough to save the money to buy a plane ticket back to California. At first, Kate thought she could live with her grandmother, but she was in a whole different school district. Better if Molly talked her parents into letting Kate live at their house.

It was only for five and a half years, just till she was out of high school. They couldn't possibly say no.

There was just one detail Kate and Molly hadn't worked out: How would Kate convince her own parents to let her come home to Isla Nada? She hoped they'd give in when they saw how miserable she was. But if they didn't, well . . .

"Hey, I tried the skates this morning at the walk," Molly was saying. "They fit if I wear two pairs of socks. I can't believe you're letting me use 'em! They are, like, way fine!"

Kate sniffled. "Well, I bet nobody in Belletoona ever heard of in-line skates. Anyway, Molly, I gotta go. Josh is supposed to come over, and . . ."

"You gotta cut out that crying before you see him, *chica*. You don't want to look all blotchy."

Kate sniffed up a tear. "I know. I hope he gets here soon. I'd *die* if I didn't get to kiss him good-bye."

Molly sighed. "I don't blame you. It must be like *heaven* to kiss him. He is, like, so—"

"Hey, Molly, will you do me a favor?"

"Well, sure, I mean—"

"Keep an eye on him for me. Deal? I trust him, but he's so gorgeous, and that Amanda girl—"

"No problem-ation, *chica*."

"Kate?" Gramma knocked on the door. "There's some *boy* here."

"Oh, gosh. Okay, but Molly—"

"Yeah?"

"One more thing. You'll think of me, won't you? Like when you're on the beach? There's no beach in Pennsylvania—"

"You bet I will! And if I find that giant whatchacallit shell you want—"

"Giant *Forreiria*—"

"I knew it sounded like a car. Anyway, I'll pack it up and send it."

They said their good-byes, and Kate turned to Gramma, still in the doorway. "Tell him I'll be there in a sec," she sniffled. "Do I look okay?"

Gramma ignored the question. "Isn't he a little old for you?"

"You sound like my *parents*." It was sort of an insult, but Gramma didn't seem to notice. Kate pinched her cheeks and ran her fingers through her blond bangs to pouf them up. "Do you have any Visine?" she asked.

"Any what?"

"Eyedrops. You know."

Her grandmother shook her head. "If he doesn't love you with red eyes, he doesn't love you at all. Now scat down the stairs. He said he couldn't stay." Kate gave her grandmother a hug, then ran downstairs to the den, where the TV was.

When she saw Josh sitting on the old love seat, she stopped. He always made her feel the same way—weak, dizzy almost, and special. He had a surfer's tan and broad shoulders, bright blue eyes, pale hair, and a brilliant smile. He ought to be *on* TV instead of watching it. How did she get so lucky?

Josh Bennett had been her boyfriend since the day in August he had kissed her outside the Shake Shack. Kate was so surprised she spilled french fries all over the walk, but he got her another order and even paid for them. He was so sweet.

Kate's parents didn't see this, though. Her dad asked why he never had any homework. Her mom was more subtle. She just "forgot" to buy Nacho Cheese Doritos, Josh's favorite, whenever she went to the store.

He looked up at her and smiled. "I can't find the remote."

"There isn't one." Kate was suddenly embarrassed by her gramma's television.

"So, like, how do you change channels?"

Kate walked over to the dial on the set to demonstrate. Josh shook his head. "Wow. Stone Age," he said.

"Is there surfing on or something?"

"Aw, that's okay, Booboo." He flashed her another heart-melting smile. "I really wanted to see *you*."

Kate sat down and leaned her head on his shoulder. For a few moments they watched a Diet Coke commercial in silence.

"I'm gonna miss ya, you know?" He ran his fingers through her hair, pulled her face over, and kissed her. Kate felt her heart thump.

"I'll miss you, too." Her voice cracked.

"Hey . . ." He moved back and looked at her. "Aw, Booboo, don't blubber. It makes your eyes all red. You'll do great there. You're tougher than you think."

She wiped a tear off her cheek and tried to smile. "And I'll be back soon."

"Sure you will, Booboo. Tough it out! Anyway, like, I'm sorry I can't hang here, but Tonio's in a rush. He'll be back in five, and we're going up the coast."

She sighed and snuggled close. "I wish this moment could last forever."

"Yeah, me—" he started, but a car horn honked outside. "Tonio." He bounced off the love seat.

"You just got here!"

Josh took both her hands and looked into her face. Kate hoped he wasn't looking at her red eyes. "I brought ya somethin'." From his back pocket he tugged a necklace made of seashells. "Hope I didn't break any sittin' on 'em."

"Oh, Josh. . . ." Kate almost lost it.

"Hey—enough o' that, Booboo. I just thought it'd look pretty on you. What kind are they, anyway?"

"Cowries," she said. "The Indians used to trade—"

The car horn interrupted her, and Josh looked out the window. "They're all snails to me. Anyway . . ."

Hand in hand, they walked to the front door. Outside, Tonio seemed to be sitting on his horn.

"I'm history," Josh said sadly. He bent his head to kiss her one more time but missed and got her nose.

As he loped down the walk, Kate hollered, "Don't forget the Valentine's dance!" She couldn't tell if he heard her or not. Fingering the cowrie necklace, she watched him climb into Tonio's Jeep, which sped away even before Josh's door was shut.

He was always racing off. One time she told him she felt like a pit stop. But he cares about me, too, she thought. When her volleyball team won the championship, he got all dressed up and took her to a steak place. She had to do some fancy talking to get permission, but finally, when she swore up and down she'd be home by eight-thirty, Mom and Dad said okay.

She could barely eat, it was so romantic — red candles, piano music, the view of waves out the window. Molly made her tell every detail on the phone afterward.

Walking home, Kate and Josh talked about the ocean, what it meant to them. Kate's grandmother had taught her about seashells and the animals that lived in them. She thought someday she might study marine biology. Josh said he wanted to own his own surf shop — maybe in Maui.

But right now, neither of them was ready to think seriously about something as overwhelming as growing up. Being a kid was too much fun.

At least it used to be. Kate clasped her new necklace around her neck, then walked over to the hall mirror to admire it. Her eyes were still red.

Three hours later, US Airways Flight 134 was over Utah, and Mom was fishing a second packet of tissues out of her purse for Kate.

"All this whimpering is getting on my nerves," Danielle said. Kate didn't answer, just wondered how she got stuck with a kid sister who talked like she was forty years old. "I'll miss *my* friends, too, you know," Danielle added.

Kate's nose was stuffed up from crying. "You dod't hab eddy fwiends—eggsept id books."

"Just 'cause *I* learned to read when *I* was four—"

"*Girls!*" Kate's mom slapped her *Gourmet* magazine shut. "I won't listen to another word! Kate, watch the movie or something. Dani, here." She pulled a fat book out of her overnight bag. "Read this."

"*Scarlet Lace?*" Danielle looked at it suspiciously. The cover showed a woman in a red nightgown reaching toward a man with an eye patch. "Is this a book for kids?"

"Read it and find out. Now be quiet."

Kate leaned back, closed her eyes and unexpectedly felt better. Ever since she first heard of Belletoona, she had been so busy fighting and crying that she hadn't stopped to ask herself why. I'm going to miss Molly and Josh, my beach, my gramma, she thought. But it's something more that has me in total panic. What?

When the answer came to her, it was simple. She was scared. Had she ever been scared before? She made a list of her life: Her mom and dad loved each other, and they loved her. She had always lived in the same house, always had the same best friend, always known every inch of the walk, the mall, and the beach, like she owned them. School wasn't too hard, and she was good at volleyball.

I mean, she thought, I even know who gives the best birthday parties and which family rooms in the neighborhood are best for snacks.

I need a pep talk, Kate thought, like Noah, our volleyball coach, used to give us at halftime. He was from New York, and he had this funny way of talking. She tried to think of his voice: "What, you're the only person in the world who's ever been scared before? Well, I got news for you! Anybody does anything new, they're gonna be sweatin' bullets! Lemme tell you something, you got nothin' to worry about! Nothin'! You got Operation Defrost! Now, get in there—"

But a real voice interrupted. "Ladies and gentlemen."

It was the pilot on the loudspeaker. "We're anticipating some turbulence as we move into the eastern United States this evening. And I hope you all brought your winter coats. The National Weather Service tells us it's thirty-six degrees and raining in Pittsburgh."

Chapter Three

Thanksgiving, Belletoona, Pennsylvania: Colder, with snow likely by nightfall.

It was going to be the worst Thanksgiving ever.

Dad had met them at the Pittsburgh airport, and they had spent the night in a hotel before driving to Belletoona on Thanksgiving morning. The route wound east through the low hills, a gray-brown landscape under a dead sky. Noah could give me all the pep talks he knows, Kate thought as she looked out the window, but they wouldn't be enough.

"You remember the downtown, don't you?" Dad asked when at last they drove into Belletoona.

"It's very charming, Father," said Danielle. Kate stuck

two fingers down her throat and gagged, but no one noticed.

Downtown Belletoona consisted of two beauty salons, a law office, a coffee shop, a bakery, and a clothing store called Mamie's. At its center was an old courthouse with a clock tower, and across from that a park with a huge pond. This was not Kate's idea of civilization. "Isn't there a McDonald's?" she asked.

"Of course! In the mall on the highway. Not far," Dad answered.

Kate thought of home, of Isla Nada. Their house—the house that *used* to be their house—was on a dead-end street with a dozen just like it, all surrounded by lawns and flowers. From it, she could walk or bike to the boardwalk—kids called it the walk—with T-shirt shops, import stores, pizza joints, and snack bars on one side and the beach on the other. Everything a kid could want was right there.

She compared the brightness of sun on sand and ocean to this place, where even the air seemed gray. At least I won't have to worry about sunscreen, she thought.

Dad steered the car right, then left, out of the downtown. Maybe it was the grayness that made Kate think of the tidal pools out by the point. She and her grandmother would leave before sunrise, when the light was dim and the air was full of fog. Every tidal pool was its own little world, Gramma had told her. They'd find anemones, which looked like flowers, and tiny pink-gray octopuses, and sea urchins, and starfish, and scads of skittering little crabs.

One time, before she knew better, Kate reached in and pulled out an octopus, all cool and slick and wriggly. Now she understood how that octopus felt—yanked right out of its world.

The car started up a hill. The houses were big and old and far apart. Most were made of gray stone. The lawns were brown, there were no flowers, and only a few stubborn dry leaves clung to the trees.

The house they had bought was the last one on the block. The real estate sign was still in the yard. Without family or furniture, Dad had stayed in a motel up till now. It would be his first night in the house, too.

The car startled an enormous black bird, which dove at it, squawking, then flew away.

"Just a crow," said Dad. "They're like seagulls. Everywhere."

No crow's that scary-looking, Kate thought. More like a *vulture*.

Mom was staring at the house. "It's right out of a storybook," she said.

Yeah, Kate thought: ghost stories.

"Isn't it?" Dad grinned. "Well, come on!"

Dad unlocked the door, and Danielle went in first. Kate had just stepped into the front hall when she heard a little shriek from her mom, then a giggle. She turned and saw that Dad had scooped Mom into his arms and was carrying her over the threshold. Talk about embarrassing! At least there was no one else around to see.

The moving van wasn't due until the next day, and the house was so empty it echoed. Mom wanted to go out to dinner, but Dad rejected that idea. He was going to cook Thanksgiving dinner himself. So the girls were left alone in the empty house while he and Mom drove around looking for an open grocery store. Danielle ran from room to room, dizzily waving her arms and humming what sounded like *The Nutcracker*. Kate sat on the bare wood floor in the living room, trying to read *Teen Surf*.

"I'm the beautiful dancing-ballerina-snowflake princess!" Danielle spun by.

Kate shook her head. How was she supposed to read? She was freezing, and in the strange house, every sound made her jump.

She had already moved the thermostat to 74. Now she went back and tried 76. She was just sitting down again when a bang reverberated through the walls.

Danielle stopped. "What was *that*?" she asked.

Kate looked around. *Bang-bang-bang!* She swallowed hard. "I don't know," she said slowly. "Probably nothing to worry about."

"Where are Mommy and Daddy?" Danielle asked. "They've been gone *forever.*"

"They'll be back," Kate said, but she was getting worried, too.

"They're *dead,*" Danielle said.

"What? No, Dani, don't be silly."

"It was too cold to drive, and the car crashed, and—"

"Look at this." Kate pulled Danielle into her lap before her morbid imagination could do more damage. It was comforting to have a warm body next to hers—even if it was the little pest.

"Isn't this guy gorgeous?" Kate pointed to a picture in the magazine.

Danielle sniffled. "He looks like Josh."

There was a tear on her sister's cheek, and Kate brushed it off. "A little," she said. "Josh is taller."

"Kate," Danielle said seriously, "do you think you'll *die* without him?"

"Where did you get an idea like that?"

"That book Mom gave me on the plane—*Scarlet Lace.* The lady got all withered up when her boyfriend joined the pirates."

"Probably I will," Kate answered. "And worms will eat me!" She made her eyes big and wiggled wormy fingers so that Danielle would know she didn't mean it.

"Eeeeeee-ew! Gross!" Danielle giggled. They both

felt better, and a few minutes later Kate heard a door close and rustling in the kitchen. Her parents were back, but they weren't talking. They must be having a fight.

"Mommy-Daddy-Mommy-Daddy!" Danielle ran in, with Kate behind her.

"Hello, pip-squeaks," Dad said. "It certainly is warm in here."

"I'm freezing," said Kate.

"Go outside," said Mom. "You'll see what freezing really is."

"I think perhaps it's going to snow soon," said Dad. "Your first snow! When you see how much fun it is, you'll be glad we left California."

"I love snow, Father," said Danielle, who had never seen it before in her life.

"Where's the turkey?" Kate asked.

Mom looked at Dad. "Uh . . . well," he answered, "the only store we could find open was Asian, and they didn't have whole turkeys. So what do you think of a stir-fried Thanksgiving dinner?"

Kate was horrified. "You're kidding, right?"

"He's not kidding," said Mom. She pulled ginger root out of the grocery bag. "See?"

"We can still have mashed potatoes," Dad said. "The store had potatoes."

"Mashed potatoes and what?" Kate asked. "Soy sauce?"

"Come on, troops," said Dad. "Where's your sense of adventure? Your esprit de corps? Your joie de vivre?"

"Where's our stuffing? Our gravy? Our cranberries?" Kate asked.

Dad ignored her. "Angela, you chop and I'll mince. This is going to be an unforgettable Thanksgiving meal."

Mom smiled in spite of herself. "Got that right."

At bedtime, Dad declared a camp-out and put their borrowed sleeping bags in the living room together. In the dark, Kate could hear her family's even breathing, but no matter how she squirmed, she couldn't get comfortable. Finally, she pulled out a flashlight, a pen and some of Gramma's stationery so she could write her first letter home.

Dear Molly,

How are you?

I am not fine.

For dinner we had to sit on the floor and eat on paper plates with plastic forks. I missed my gramma and even my fat uncle Tom—the one in the car commercials?—who always eats with us. Plus it would have been nice to have a chair. Plus I was freezing.

Then the doorbell rang and it was Mr. Douglas. He sold us our house, and it turns out he lives across the street. He invited us over to eat dessert, and when we got there and his wife found out about our dinner, she gave us turkey and everything so at least that was really nice. And the pumpkin pie was yum. Mom said Mrs. Douglas even made the crust herself, which Mom said is amazing.

Mr. and Mrs. Douglas have a son and he hardly looked at me—just played Gameboy (snore). He's a year older than me, 13, so he goes to the middle school (that's what they call junior high here), so I guess I won't ever see him, which is good since I'm going to be a nun. I think his name is Peter.

Mr. and Mrs. Douglas were all, "Are you looking forward to starting school next week, dear?" and "Do you miss your friends?" and "How do you like this cold weather?" They were being nice so I tried to be nice back. Mostly Dani and I watched TV, which was all football, and it was so boring, and I felt lonely and thought about last year after Thanksgiving dinner when we all went down to the walk and hung out and bought that pizza, like just what we needed! More food!

Now it's actually snowing! I didn't know snow was so dry, not like rain at all. It is really—omigosh, I almost called it cool! *Get it? Well, it is. Pretty, too, the way it swirls in the air and turns the trees all soft and white.*

Oh gross, now I'm all poetic.

Keep working on your parents about Operation Defrost. And keep an eye on Josh.

Your best friend,

Kate

P.S. — I almost forgot! Walking home tonight I saw the weirdest thing — a phantom! No lie! This sort of white flash — like a cross between a snowball and a meteor — streaked by our house. Nobody else saw it, so now they think I'm crazy.

P.P.S. — Write to me!

Chapter Four

Friday, November 28, Belletoona, Pennsylvania: Snow continuing today and Saturday.

Kate woke up when Dad shook her shoulder the next morning. She mumbled something grumpy and tried to curl back into her sleeping bag, but Dad was persistent. "Come on, pip-squeak," he said. "It's beautiful outside. Like fairyland."

Kate opened her eyes a slit and peered through her lashes out the window. The trees, the lawn — everything glowed white against the gray sky. It was so beautiful she opened her eyes the rest of the way.

"It reminds me of when I was a boy in Buffalo," Dad was saying. "We'd build snowmen and go ice-skating and sledding. The best times of my life were in the winter."

Kate rolled her eyes. Dad would never understand about California. Maybe you had to be born there.

It was late, and Danielle was already up, too. Wearing her bathrobe, she twirled around the sleeping bags and sang about the beautiful dancing-ballerina-snowflake princess. Kate could see there was no point in trying to go back to sleep.

"What time's the moving van coming?" she asked.

"It was scheduled for eight, but with this weather, I'm not surprised he's late."

Kate and Danielle ate leftover rice sitting cross-legged on the floor by the dining room windows. The snow in the air looked like sifted sugar. Kate could hardly bear to think how cold it must be. You'd be crazy to go outside, she thought.

An hour later, she was layering cold-weather gear — long underwear, wool socks, turtleneck, sweater, coat, hat, mittens — onto her body.

"You can't stay in an empty house all day," said Mom as she tied her own hood.

Kate zipped her hideous red coat, a hand-me-down from her cousins in Buffalo. She couldn't believe what a pain it was just to go outside. No wonder it took polar explorers so long to get anywhere. Admiral Peary must have spent most of his time getting dressed.

Mom opened the door just as the moving van pulled up to the curb. In the gust of freezing air, Kate announced, "I will never be warm again." Danielle pushed her aside and bounded out with her mouth open to catch snowflakes.

Reluctantly, Kate followed, just in time to hear a squeal as a car braked abruptly. The van was so big, drivers couldn't see around it to the stop sign on the corner. Another squeal, and a second car skidded on the snowy street, barely avoiding a collision.

"Glad *I* don't have to drive in this weather," said Mom.

The same man who took the furniture and boxes out of their house in Isla Nada had brought them across country, and here he was again, coming up the walk. Ridiculously, Kate felt glad to see him—a link to life in California, to her real life. He nodded to Mom and slapped his gloved hands together. "Quite a drive with the snow," he said. "I've got a couple guys on the way to help. I wanna get this over with, get home to Florida. I don't have any use for cold."

His name was Jack Burns, Kate remembered. Now she watched him go back to the van, open up the side doors and yank down the ramp. A few minutes later, a pickup truck pulled up, and a couple more men got out.

All day long, it was a parade on the front walk—chair, mattress, table, sofa, box, box, box. Kate helped, and in spite of her prediction, she was soon warm. She found she even enjoyed the flying flakes. It was like being inside a Christmas globe. The trickiest thing was staying upright. Scrunched by Kate's footsteps, the snow made a layer of ice on the soles of her boots. Each time she stepped over the threshold onto the wood floor, she slid.

Meanwhile, Danielle fell *thump* on her bottom twice and had hysterics the second time. Maybe she isn't quite so in love with the snow anymore, Kate thought.

At dusk the two guys in the pickup truck pulled out of the driveway, and Jack Burns carried the last box up the icy walk. It was covered with red Fragile stickers. "I'll take that one," Kate said.

When she reached for it, her boot slipped, and she went down on one knee. Mr. Burns grabbed her elbow. "Steady, there. Be a shame to break anything that's come so far," he said.

Kate found her footing. "It's my seashell collection."

"Better take good care of 'em then," said Mr. Burns. "You won't be findin' seashells around here."

Kate didn't answer, just turned and carried her treasure into the house, up the stairs, and to the front bedroom on the right. Even though her bed was in it, and her desk and her dresser, she told herself this was the guest room.

She unwrapped the tissue around each shell and placed them on top of her dresser: bubble shells, limpets, a piddock, scallops, sand dollars, a murex. Some she had found, and others she had bought at a shop on the walk. None had broken. When they were arranged, she put a big conch up to her ear and closed her eyes so that she could listen to the ocean. For a moment, she was sitting

on the sand with her friends, watching Josh ride the
waves. She knew she was really hearing the echo of blood
pulsing in her own head, but she could pretend, couldn't
she?

"I'll fix you some hot chocolate," Mom said. How long
had she been standing in the doorway? "Mr. Burns
wouldn't take any. He's already in the truck, warming up
the turbo, whatever that is."

Kate put her shell down. "We don't have cocoa mix, do
we?" she said. "Unless you got it at the Asian grocery
store."

"They had real cocoa, the bitter kind."

"Do you know how to make hot chocolate that way?"

"Kate! Of course I do! Anyway, the directions are on
the package."

Kate followed her mother down to the kitchen. Even
from here, at the back of the house, she could hear the
rumble of the moving van's engine warming up. Danielle
was already sitting at the table expectantly. There were
packing boxes on the counters and the floor, but Mom
cleared a space and found what she needed. After a few
minutes, looking pleased with herself, she poured steam-
ing liquid into mugs.

"It's good, Mom," Kate said.

"Yes, Mother. I can't believe it," said Danielle.

"I might even learn to bake bread," said Mom. Kate
almost dropped her mug. "Why not?" Mom asked. "I

won't be working right away. Homey pursuits might agree with me."

"Is that one of Father's ideas?" Danielle was suspicious.

"No, it is not. It's my own idea."

Homey was not a word Kate thought of when she thought of Mom. In California, Mom commuted to L.A. to work every day. She wore short skirts, big earrings, and bangle bracelets. As for cooking . . . Kate tried to think . . . Mom *did* make guacamole from real avocados. Other than that, they ate a lot of Froot Loops, takeout pizza, Campbell's Soup, and Chinese.

Kate remembered the *Gourmet* magazine on the airplane. I guess this homey thing is her way of making the best of things, Kate thought. But Mom wearing an apron? Up to her elbows in flour and dough? No way.

Kate was rinsing her mug when there was a clatter of gears shifting, and the rumble became a squeal. "What was *that*?" she asked.

"Just Mr. Burns pulling out," said her mom. But the next noise was terrible: screaming tires and the engine's roar. All three of them hurried to the window and looked into the night. The moving van, its red and yellow lights illuminating the snow, inched forward, then lurched back, giant tires spinning.

Mom put on her coat and carried one of Dad's snow shovels—the hall closet was full of snow shovels—out to

Mr. Burns. Kate watched him use it to chip ice and snow from around the tires, but it didn't work. The enormous moving van was stuck in front of the house.

"Roads are awful. Sorry I'm late," Dad said when he came in a few minutes later. "What's Burns still doing out there?"

Mom explained.

"Do invite him in, at least," Dad said.

"He won't come. Says he's got everything he needs— phone, VCR, bed—right there in the cab. He says he'll just wait for the spring thaw."

"Ha-ha. Amusing fellow," said Dad. "I'll bring him in. Who could resist leftover Thanksgiving stir-fry?"

Whether it was the stir-fry or the promise of a fire in the fireplace, Mr. Burns was soon stomping his snow-covered boots by the front door. "Isn't this the pits?" he said. "I don't see how people stand it all winter long. Sure glad I live in Florida." No one said anything, and Mr. Burns went on quickly. "Oh, well . . . I mean it's great for *some* people. I'm sure there's a lotta good to say about a Pennsylvania winter. Whole lotta good."

Dad raised one eyebrow, which usually meant he thought something was funny but the wrong kind of funny for a smile. "You've had a long drive and a difficult day, Mr. Burns," he said. "Come in and sit down awhile. Dinner won't take a minute."

In the living room, Dad arranged kindling and Mom sat across from Mr. Burns on the sofa. Kate and Danielle perched on boxes.

"Where're you from originally, ma'am?" Mr. Burns asked Mom.

"Southern California, born and bred."

"How d'you like this weather?"

"Well, I'm not sure," she answered. "I do like the beach and being outdoors in the sunshine . . ." Dad, kneeling on the hearth, looked over his shoulder and caught her eye. "But I suppose I can take up winter sports," she added quickly. "Skiing and, uh . . . sledding. And I thought I might do a little cooking . . ."

"Eating, too, no doubt," Mr. Burns answered. "Cold always makes a body hungry. You'll bulk up just like a polar bear."

Mom looked horrified, and Kate wondered if she were wishing they'd left Mr. Burns out in his truck. "Uh . . . do you have a profession, ma'am?" he asked after a minute.

"I'm a film editor. Commercials. Industrial productions. That kind of thing."

"Wouldn't think they'd do much o' *that* in Belletoona," said Mr. Burns.

There was a moment's silence, then Dad sat back on his heels and grinned. "Look at my fire." It had crackled to life.

Mom smiled. "Oh, isn't that nice!" But a second later,

a puff of smoke blew into the room, then another and another.

"Did you check the damper?" Mr. Burns asked between coughs.

Dad stuck his head into the fireplace. "Open." He coughed.

"I think I'll finish up dinner." Mom headed for the kitchen.

Kate followed. As she folded paper towels into napkins, she overheard Mr. Burns say, "Probably just bats in the chimney."

Oh, *great*, thought Kate. A vulture. A ghost. A phantom. Now *bats*.

While Dad doused the fire and Mom heated up dinner, Danielle performed her dancing-ballerina-snowflake-princess dance for Mr. Burns. That oughta pay him back for the cracks about polar bears, Kate thought. They had finally sat down and Mr. Burns was exclaiming over the unusual leftovers when the squeal of brakes and a terrible crash interrupted him. "My rig!" he shouted, jumping up.

Everyone was right behind him, but before they reached the door, there was another crash, then another.

What in the world was happening?

Even after the door was open and they were all standing, coatless and cold, in the snowy front yard, it took a while to comprehend the chaos in the street. The moving van was still there, massive and undisturbed. But beyond it were cars, lots of cars, their headlights and taillights pointing every which way, their doors open, their drivers standing beside them or on the curb. Some were shouting, others just shaking their heads.

While Kate and her family watched, another car came barreling down the street, slammed on its brakes, skidded on the snow, and slid—*crash*—into the pileup.

Danielle was the first to speak. "Wow," she said. "Do you think living here will always be this exciting?"

When Kate lay down for the first time in her old bed in her new room—the guest room, that is—she realized she was even more lonely than tired. It was three hours earlier in California, so she picked up the phone to call Molly.

"Just a second," said a voice before she even dialed. "Kate?"

"Oh, sorry, Mom," she mumbled. She hung up, wondering who Mom needed to talk to. She can't be lonely. She has Dad, not to mention Dani and me.

Kate waited a couple of minutes and picked up the phone again, but Mom was still there. And she sounded crabbier this time. Molly would probably think Kate was crazy, writing two letters in two days. But she had to talk to somebody.

Dear Molly,

Remember when we had omen *as a vocabulary word? Well, I don't know, but it doesn't seem like a good omen that half the cars in our neighborhood crashed into the other half right in front of our house on our first whole day in Belletoona.*

The police left a little while ago.

They were pretty nice. They said the moving van was parked legally and it wasn't really Mr. Burns's fault no one could see the stop sign, which is what caused the chain reaction. Well, that and all the snow.

Then they called this enormo truck to come and tow the van because the tires were half buried in ice. Mr. Burns was really glad to be headed back to Florida, even though he never did get to eat his dinner.

Like always, Dad said look at the bright side, and I'm thinking, if I look at the bright side any more I'll be blind. He is always such an optimist (we had that word the same week we had omen, *remember?), which Mom says is good, but I'm not so sure. Anyway, he said nobody was hurt, and we got to meet the neighbors when they came in to use our phone. Some of them weren't in very good moods though. One guy, he was short and pretty old with a beard, he was all "Oooooh, my neck!" and talking about how some rel-*

ative is a big lawyer in Philadelphia. It's lucky Mom learned to make hot chocolate today. They drank a lot.

Mr. Douglas came over after to make sure we were okay. He brought his son who actually spoke to me! He said it never snows this much in November. I think he wants to be a TV weatherman when he grows up.

Your best friend,

Kate

P.S.—Write and tell me how it's going with your parents and Operation Defrost.

P.P.S.—It's still snowing.

Chapter Five

Snowfall sets November record
Satellite reveals Arctic storm approaching
THE BELLETOONA *Bugle*, SATURDAY, NOVEMBER 29

In the middle of the night, Kate was awakened by a noise she had never heard before: *crunch-SCRA-A-A-APE, crunch-SCRA-A-A-APE, crunch-SCRA-A-A-APE.*

She rolled over and looked at the clock radio: 3:22.

"Katie-e-e-e, Katie-e-e-e? Are you awake? There's something out there! Something with long bloody fingernails climbing up the house!" Danielle was standing at the foot of the bed.

The noise stopped, and Kate, a little shaky, climbed

out of bed, took her sister's hand and walked with her to the front window.

Across the street, a dark hooded figure was standing on the sidewalk. "An ax murderer!" Danielle gasped.

Kate was spooked, too. Should she call 9-1-1? Yell for Daddy?

The ominous stranger bend down to resume his work. *Crunch-SCRA-A-A-APE.*

"He's digging something," Kate whispered.

"A grave!" Danielle's eyes were wide.

Kate tried to sound brave. "That's ridiculous, Dani. Nobody'd dig a grave in the middle of the sidewalk." Would they?

Crunch-SCRA-A-A-APE, crunch-SCRA-A-A-APE. The figure stopped again, raised his arms over his head, and turned toward the window where the girls stood. Simultaneously, they jumped back and yelled:

"Daddy!"

"Mommy-Daddy! Help!"

There was a thump down the hall, garbled muttering, running footsteps. Then Daddy was beside them. "What'sa matter? What are you doing up?"

Kate could hardly make her tongue form words, "Something . . . someone . . . *gravedigger!*"

"Huh?" Dad looked out. Then, to Kate's amazement, he grinned. "Hey! It's one of ours. The new Flying Penguin model."

Kate started breathing again, but Danielle still didn't get it. "It's Mr. Douglas," Dad explained. "He's using one of our new shovels." The figure stretched one more time, then went back to work. *Crunch-SCRA-A-A-APE, crunch-SCRA-A-A-APE.*

Nobody slept well after that. By seven-thirty, the family was eating breakfast. The sky had cleared, and the sun was just beginning to illuminate the snow. "It *is* beautiful," Mom said. "Like fairyland."

After a half hour of finding and layering clothes, Dad gathered the family on the front porch. Then he picked up a snow shovel and cleared his throat. "Before we get to work," he said, "I'd like to say a few words about the implement we'll be using, the implement commonly called the snow shovel. As most of you know, your snow shovel differs from your dirt shovel in regard to several basic points. I'll take them one at a time, beginning at the blade and working my way north, to the handle. Please hold your questions."

As Dad talked, a woman came out of the house next door and stood in her yard, watching. A minute later, Mr. Douglas came out of his house, too. Great, Kate thought. Soon the whole neighborhood will be listening to Dad's lecture on the common snow shovel. They'll think we're crazy.

"Dad," she interrupted, "don't you think we could get started?"

"Really, Coldwell," Mom chimed in. "How complicated can it be?" Dad looked crushed. "We're just so very eager to give our new snow shovels a try," Mom added.

"Yeah, Dad," said Kate. "We don't want the snow to melt first."

"All right," Dad said reluctantly. "But let me leave you with three final words to shovel by: *Bend your knees.*"

Dad passed out shovels, a small pink one for Danielle and regular-size black-and-white Flying Penguin models for Mom and Kate. Then he gave each person an assignment. "We'll reconnoiter back here at oh-nine-thirty," he said.

"Roger wilco, dear," said Mom.

As they walked off, Kate heard Danielle whisper, "Dad was never in the army, was he?"

Mom shook her head. "No, but he's seen a *lot* of war movies."

The storm had left about ten inches of snow. Kate found it took two scoopfuls—top layer, bottom layer—to clear one patch of sidewalk. Bend-and-toss, bend-and-toss, she soon got into a rhythm. While she worked, she thought of Josh and Molly. It was five-thirty in the morning in Isla Nada. Josh would be tugging on his wet suit. Molly would be asleep for hours yet. If I were there, Kate thought, I'd call her about noon and maybe talk her into hunting seashells or going for a swim.

Kate missed her beach already. She loved the way the

sand squeaked beneath her toes, the cries of the seabirds, the rush and retreat of the waves that went on forever. Bend-and-toss, bend-and-toss—shoveling made her think of the sand toys she played with when she was little. The beach had always been part of her life.

I bet Molly won't even go down there today, Kate thought. She'll check out the shops on the walk or beg her mom for a ride to the mall. Molly was her best friend—always there in a pinch, always cheerful—but she liked to shop way more than Kate did. I mean, Kate thought, there are only so many nail polish colors you can buy, only so many nachos you can eat, only so many earrings you can wear, even if, like Molly, you do have four holes in each ear.

Bend-and-toss, bend-and-toss. Kate looked up, and there was Mr. Douglas. "Little more arc on the upswing," he suggested. "You don't want your banks to collapse. Is your dad around? I gave that new shovel of his a shakedown cruise early this A.M."

"I know," Kate said.

"I like to get a jump on it," he said. "Wouldn't have one of those snowblowers, though. *Those'll* wake the dead."

"Here I am, Douglas." Dad came around the side of the house. "That Flying Penguin do okay by you?"

As Mr. Douglas described his shoveling experience, the woman next door reemerged from her house, carrying a plate in one hand and a squirming red bundle under her arm. "Good morning!" She high-stepped awkwardly toward them through the snow. "Weather gave you a warm welcome, eh? I'm Tonya Mooney. We met last night—the blue Eldorado?"

Dad shook his head. "I'm sorry, there were so many . . ."

"Right, right. Doesn't matter. Fender'll be straightened out one o' these days. You folks're from California, eh? Saw the license plates. Welcome to Society Hill."

"Society Hill?" Kate looked at her dad, but he was puzzled, too.

"Oh, that's just what the folks down in town call it," Mrs. Mooney explained. "Rumor is we're the well-to-do up here." The squirmy thing squirmed again, and Kate realized it was a kid plumped up in a red snowsuit. Boy or girl, she couldn't tell.

Mrs. Mooney held out the plate of cookies. "Help yourself," she said. "They're right out of the oven. Say . . ."

Mrs. Mooney looked at Kate critically. "The girl who sits for me, Tiffany her name is, she's gone and gotten herself a boyfriend—can you imagine? And she's your age? Anyhow, she always claims she's busy. Do you baby-sit?"

On cue, the red-snowsuit kid squawked, "Dow', dow', dow'!" Mrs. Mooney leaned over and dropped it into the soft snow, where it sank to its knees.

Kate hesitated, but Dad answered, "She baby-sits her little sister all the time."

"I can use a good baby-sitter," said Mrs. Mooney. "If you're not busy next Saturday, my husband and I are going to a party. What do you say?"

The offer was almost drowned out by the howls of Red-Suit, who had fallen flat after trying to take a step in the snow. Mrs. Mooney never stopped talking, just scooped the child up, brushed off the snow, and put it back down. "Nicky never cries," she said. Kate wondered who Nicky was, then realized it must be Red-Suit, even though he was crying at that moment. "He's a very easy baby."

Kate had never baby-sat a kid that little before, but here was her chance to start earning money for the airfare home—a chance dropped right in her lap. Besides, Mom and Dad would be next door if she needed to bail out, or—gross—change a diaper. "Okay," she said. She smiled at Nicky, whose eyes she could just see between his stocking cap and his scarf. He peered at her suspiciously, took a step backward, sat down in the snow, and started to scream again.

Mrs. Mooney didn't blink, just threw him over her shoulder and hauled him toward home. "Great meeting you," she called.

* * *

"You promised!" It was a little after dinner—Kate couldn't believe stir-fried turkey had lasted three whole nights. Dad was standing ankle-deep in packing peanuts, undoing the bubble wrap around some saucers. Kate had teacup duty. " 'You can call your friends whenever you want,' that's what you *said*! 'Don't worry about the long-distance,' that's what you *said*! You're a—a—" Kate had never called her dad a name before, at least not a name as bad as *liar*, and the word wouldn't quite come out now.

"Settle down, pip-squeak. I am quite aware of my promises. But your mother wants to talk to Gramma. When she's done—"

"Are you kidding? They'll yak all night! Just lemme call Josh one minute and—"

"Too late." Danielle, the dancing-ballerina-snowflake princess, spun by and pointed at Mom, unpacking silverware in the dining room. The phone was already to her ear.

"*Oh!*" In frustration, Kate slammed down a cup, which broke neatly in half.

Later, when she finally did get to call, she told Josh about it. "I, like, thought Daddy was gonna ground me or something."

"Aw, Booboo, don't feel bad." Josh was crunching on something. Kate could picture him perfectly, sitting on the green sofa in his family room, a bowl of Nacho Cheese Doritos in his lap. "Didn't you tell me there was nothing to do there? And you don't know anybody yet. So, like, it's sort of a good time to be grounded." *Crunch crunch.*

"I guess," said Kate, but she wasn't convinced.

"Hey, remember that dude who promised to take me to Pismo sometime?"

Kate didn't. "Yeah, sure."

"Well, I saw him today and he promised again. Soon. Like, I'd be so stoked to go up there."

Kate sighed. She didn't feel like talking about surfing. "It all seems so far away."

"Yeah, I guess it would. But they surf back there, you know. At Hatteras and someplace in New Jersey. Isn't New Jersey sort of near you?" *Crunch crunch.*

"Sort of, I think."

"Be right with ya!" he called to somebody. "Well, look, Booboo, I really gotta go. Justin's here, and we're meeting some of the dudes on the walk to maybe get snacks or something. You know."

"Josh?"

Crunch, crunch. "Yeah?"

"Do you miss me?"

"Well . . . yeah. Sure, Booboo. I sit out there on my board and I look for you on the beach, and then it's like, oh yeah—she's *gone.* Like, *shoot.* I mean, I'm *devastated.*"

Kate sniffed the tears back. "Me too."

When Josh hung up, Kate held on to the phone and listened to the silence. I am going to be a nun, she told herself. I only hope Josh is, too.

Chapter Six

Monday, December 1, Belletoona, Pennsylvania: Colder, chance of snow by nightfall.

"Tell me again why there's no school today," Danielle asked her dad. They had spent all day Sunday unpacking boxes, and Dad had taken today off to work on house stuff, too. Now, for a break, they were building a snowman in the front yard.

"First day of deer-hunting season," he answered. Danielle must have gotten warm rolling snowballs in the sunshine, because she had taken off her coat and hat. They made a perfect outfit for the snowman, with her snowboots for feet.

"That's a holiday? For deer hunting?" Kate said from the doorway. She had no intention of leaving the warm house that day, but her mom had told her to go ask the builders if they were ready for hot chocolate.

"Fine sport," said her dad. "Maybe we'll go out ourselves next year."

"You mean *shoot Bambi*?" Danielle was horrified.

Kate thought it made perfect sense that the people around here went deer hunting. It snowed all the time, the mall was dinky, and there was no ocean. After a while, anybody would want to go out in the woods and kill something.

She was grateful for the extra day off, though. Being cooped up in refrigerator-land with her family was boring but safe. She and her mom had even had a good talk while they hammered nails in the walls for pictures. It turned out Mom *was* lonely. Still, Kate figured Mom's problems were nothing compared to hers. Mom didn't have to start school tomorrow.

Mr. Douglas had been out scraping ice off the windshield of his car. Now he came over to admire the snowman and warn the neighbors that more "white stuff" was on the way. "A piece of advice for the newcomers," he said. "Keep on top of the shoveling. Get behind, ya got ice to contend with. Sure is pretty now though, isn't it? Like fairyland."

Kate thought if she heard one more person say "like fairyland," she would barf.

*   *   *

Mr. Douglas's prediction was right, and snow began falling that evening. Sometime before dawn, Kate was awakened again by *crunch-SCRA-A-A-APE*. Even though she knew what it was, she got up and looked out the window. As she watched, the familiar sound was interrupted by a loud snap. It was hard to see what had happened, but then Mr. Douglas raised his hands, and there was a piece of snow shovel in each. The Flying Penguin had broken in two.

Too much arc on the upswing, Kate thought.

She was just turning away when something else caught her eye, a white streak that shot past Danielle's snowman and disappeared around the side of the house. The phantom snowball!

What could it be? There were big, fat squirrels everywhere, but squirrels slept at night like people, didn't they? Anyway, squirrels were gray. Kate padded back to bed, but as soon as she lay down, the walls echoed: *bang-bang-bang*. As she lay there, her stomach began to knot up. She knew she wasn't sick. Her stomach felt like it did when she had a dentist appointment—worried. A wave of questions washed over her. Would school be hard? Would the kids be cliquey? What was she supposed to talk to them about? Bambi? The weather? She half wished Peter across the street was a year younger so he'd be in the elementary school, too. It would be nice to recognize somebody. Even somebody who hardly talked.

Mom had made her lay out clothes the night before—
long underwear, of course, and jeans, a turtleneck, a
Pacific-blue sweatshirt with *Isla Nada* printed on the
back. Do kids even dress like this here? she wondered.
Maybe the girls wear plaid jumpers and tights and loafers.

There was so much to worry about.

For some reason, Kate thought of Amanda, who had
moved to Isla Nada at the end of last summer. Had she
been nice to Amanda? Not nice and not mean, she decided. Amanda was cute and knew how to spike a volleyball. She had come from San Francisco or someplace and
wore these old-time hippie-type clothes that Kate and
Molly agreed were totally ugly. Some of Josh's friends had
noticed her anyway, and Kate had felt a stab of jealousy
when she saw the smile Josh gave her the first time she
came into the Shake Shack.

Now Kate wished she had been nicer to the new girl.

The next thing Kate knew, Mom was waking her. It was
still dark, but the streetlamp revealed yesterday's snowman, now a shapeless lump under a layer of new snow.
Where his face used to be, there was only the orange tip
of his carrot nose.

Dad, she saw, was already out in the driveway with his
snow shovel. A few flakes flurried around him, but the sky
was becoming pearly.

"Hurry up!" Mom called. "Oatmeal's getting cold."

Oatmeal?

Downstairs, Danielle was sitting at the kitchen table, which was set like they were going to have dinner—cloth napkins, even.

"What is going on?" Kate whispered. "Are we having company to breakfast?"

"I think maybe the snow is making Mother crazy," Danielle whispered back. "I saw it on TV. Snow made this whole family crazy. In the end, they ate each other."

"Well, *we* are going to eat oatmeal with brown sugar and raisins," said Mom, who had overheard. "And I made hot chocolate."

Kate thought the oatmeal was pretty good, once she decided the lumps were supposed to be there. Danielle took a couple of bites, then set her spoon down.

"Didn't like it?" Mom had been watching them eat.

"Oh no, Mother, I *loved* it," she said. "I loved it so much I'm going to save the rest."

Dad came in carrying a broken snow shovel. When he stomped his feet, clumps of snow scattered over the kitchen floor, instantly melting into puddles. Mom didn't say anything, just scowled and got a mop from the broom closet.

"Did that one break, too?" Kate asked him.

"What do you mean?" he answered. "I found it on the front porch."

"It must be Mr. Douglas's," she explained. "I saw him break one last night."

Dad studied the pieces, then shook his head. "Improper technique. Only explanation. Still, I better take him a new one. Can't have a dissatisfied customer."

When the floor was dry, Mom served Dad his breakfast and watched him take a bite. The oatmeal had cooled, and Dad had trouble swallowing.

"How do you like it?" Mom asked.

"Great," Dad said thickly. "Only . . . Well, I'd grown so accustomed to Froot Loops."

After breakfast, Kate began the long process of suiting up: gloves, hat, muffler, snow boots, and the hideous red coat.

"Mom, can we *please* buy me a new coat at least?" she asked.

Mom ran her finger down a fraying seam. "It is a little mothy-looking . . ."

"What's the matter with it?" Dad broke in. "When I was a boy, I had one just like it."

"Daddy, I look like a blood blister," Kate said. She was about to add something she'd be grounded for when Danielle saved her.

"I can't find *anything*!" she howled from her room.

Mom looked at her watch and ran up the stairs. Great, thought Kate. On top of everything, we're going to be late. Nothing like making an entrance. "Well, when did you have them last?" Kate heard her mom saying. "When you were outside yesterday? And then what did you do with them?"

"Oh *no*," Dad groaned, and Mom came barreling down the stairs. "The snowman!" they both said at once.

Dad ran out the door and started batting snow from the top of the lump that used to be the snowman. Soon he had freed Danielle's hat, and coat, both frozen stiff. Then he dug out her boots, which were filled with powdery snow.

"There's no time to dry them," said Mom. "You'll just have to wear my extra hat and my white jacket. Maybe my boots will go over your shoes—"

"I will *not*," Danielle said.

Mom looked at her watch again. "Honey, you've got to be reasonable. School starts in ten minutes."

"I will *not*." She stamped her foot.

"What do we do?" Mom turned to Dad.

"You're asking me?"

"Well, it's *your* fault."

Daddy raised one eyebrow. "Let's not fight, Angela."

"You always say that when I'm right."

Kate's parents glared at each other. Then Mom's mouth pursed, and Daddy laughed. Danielle tried to duck, but Daddy was faster. He pushed Mom's hat down over Danielle's ears and wrapped Mom's coat around her. Even Kate felt bad for the total pest. She looked like a dandelion puff.

They drove the slick mile to Byrd Elementary School and pulled into the lot five minutes late. "Come on," Mom said. "Dad can park and follow us."

When Kate caught sight of herself in the glass entrance doors, she silently said a prayer: Oh, please, let all the girls in the sixth grade have enormous, red, hand-me-down coats.

Then Mom pushed the door open and motioned Kate inside. Danielle, waddling and half blind in Mom's coat and hat, brought up the rear.

"Awfully quiet," said Mom as they walked down the hallway. "Kids here must be very studious."

There's nothing else to do, thought Kate.

No one was behind the counter in the office. "Hello?" Mom called. After a moment, a man's voice answered, "Be right with you."

A minute passed. Was the school haunted or something? There should be people around someplace. Kate looked at her mom, who shrugged, and at Danielle—but she was invisible underneath the too-big clothes. Finally-there were footsteps, and a short man with a beard appeared. His neck was in a brace. Kate thought the man looked familiar, but it took her a second to realize from where.

Then she recognized him. Oh *no*! What was *he* do-ing . . . ?

"I'm Doyle Payne, the principal here at Byrd Elementary," he said. "I'd shake your hand, Mrs. Sommers, but I'm not sure my lawyer would approve."

"Your lawyer?" Mom looked confused, but then, like Kate, she realized where she had seen this bearded man before. He was the groaner from the accident the other night, the one who had said some relative was a lawyer in Philadelphia. "I-I'm so sorry," Mom stammered. "I didn't realize you were hurt badly enough to—"

"I don't think we'd better discuss it." He acted stuck-up. "My lawyer is drafting the paperwork," he went on. "In the meantime, I don't expect the education of your daughters to be adversely impacted. I'm a very fair man." The way he said it made Kate think *un*fair was more like it. Now she not only had the other kids to worry about, she had the principal himself.

Who would her teacher turn out to be? Dracula?

There were footsteps in the hallway, and her dad walked in the door behind them. He took one look at Mr. Payne and said, "Oh dear." Mr. Payne just arched his eyebrows. "Look," Dad began, "the van was parked legally, the police said so, and—"

Mr. Payne put up his hand to signal for silence. "As I was just telling your lovely wife, my lawyer will be in touch."

"He's the principal," Mom whispered to Dad. Then, in a normal voice, "Shouldn't we get these girls to class, Doyle? It's getting late."

"I'm sorry. Most of our families have radio or television," Mr. Payne said. "Don't you?"

"Well, naturally," Dad answered, "but I don't see what that—"

"—because it was on *all* the stations this morning," the principal said. "School is canceled today. Last night's snowfall. Not all the roads are clear for the buses."

"Yippee!" There was a muffled cry from the puffball.

"By the way, Mrs. Sommers," the stuffy voice followed them into the hallway. "I expect a degree of formality in my position. Children *and* parents call me Mr. Payne."

Chapter Seven

Wednesday, December 3, Belletoona, Pennsylvania: Unseasonably cold.

Kate prayed for snow, but she didn't get lucky twice. When she came downstairs Wednesday morning, Mom had the radio on: "Belletoona schools are on a regular schedule today after yesterday's closure," the guy was saying. "District officials decline to comment about the possibility of curtailing spring vacation in the event of an unusual number of snow days."

"What was that?" Kate sat down. Cloth napkins again, she noticed. And maple syrup on the table.

"If they close school for snow too much, they cut vacations." Dad looked over the edge of the newspaper. "One year in Buffalo it snowed so much we were still in school Fourth of July."

Danielle looked at her mom. "Father's fibbing, right?"

"Hard to tell," said Mom. She slid pancakes onto each plate. "Eat."

Kate stuck her fork into the first pancake and a white gob of raw batter oozed out around it. She gulped and put her fork down. Danielle looked horrified.

"Uh . . . I'm not that hungry, Mom," Kate said. "I think I'll just drink the hot chocolate."

"What's wrong with the pancakes?" Mom asked.

"They're delicious, Mother," said Danielle. "I'm going to save mine for later."

"Shall I put them with your oatmeal from yesterday?"

Danielle missed the sarcasm. "Excellent idea," she said.

Mom looked over Daddy's shoulder. He had pushed his plate back, too. "All right, Coldwell, what's the matter with them?"

"It's not that we don't appreciate hot breakfasts," Daddy began, "it's just that . . . Perhaps you're being too ambitious. Perhaps you should start with frozen waffles and work up."

"Tomorrow morning," Mom announced, "Froot Loops."

As Kate tugged on her boots, she heard the radio in the

kitchen. ". . . clear skies today. Currently it's thirteen degrees in Belletoona."

"That's snowsuit weather." Mom held up a plump, purple coverall for Danielle. "Come on, honey. Let's see if we can stuff you into this thing. I only wish we had one for Kate, too."

"You look like a grape with arms," Kate said when Mom was finished zipping, snapping, and tying Danielle into it. Danielle stuck out her tongue.

But a moment later the laugh was on Kate. She wouldn't have believed she could be colder than she had already been. But today the cold penetrated the red coat and went straight for her bones. It numbed her nose, stung her eyes, and turned her silver earrings into shards of ice that froze her earlobes. Danielle waddled past: "I'm toasty warm," she said to Kate.

"Stick out your tongue again, pest. Maybe it'll freeze."

Byrd Elementary School was a lot livelier today. To avoid Mr. Payne, Mom had decided to skip the office and find Kate's classroom herself. Meanwhile, Dad was escorting Danielle.

Being in a hallway choked with kids reminded Kate of her old school, only everything was just a little different, like a blurry picture of something familiar. It was confusing. She kept thinking she should recognize the kids or the teachers, but she didn't. In Isla Nada, the paintings outside the kindergarten classroom were fish; here there were paintings, too, but they were snowmen. Even the smell was the same but not the same. Disinfectant and chalk dust and mushy cafeteria vegetables—like every school on the planet. But in Isla Nada you couldn't escape the salty smell of the ocean. Here there was something sharp and metallic in the air. Did snow and ice have a smell?

Kate's stomach started worrying again. "Mom, wait a minute," she said. "I . . . I think I have to go to the bathroom."

Mom raised her eyebrows—she knows I'm stalling, Kate thought—but she said, "Go ahead, honey."

There was no one else in the restroom, and Kate stared at herself in the mirror. What will the kids here think of me? she wondered. They won't know I used to be the class president, that I have a cute boyfriend, that people like me. All they'll know is I've got blond hair and a hideous red coat.

She heard the click of the hall door opening, and she quickly turned the water on. In walked a petite girl her own age with straight brown hair and a perfect little face—the kind of girl that always made Kate feel huge and gawky, like an overgrown golden retriever. At least this girl was wearing jeans—not a plaid jumper. Her coat was plum-colored.

The girl looked at Kate without smiling, then disappeared into one of the stalls. In a moment, Kate smelled a burning match, then the acrid-sweet stink of cigarette smoke. She wrinkled her nose. *That's no different than Isla Nada. Even Molly used to smoke sometimes—until Kate convinced her it was disgusting.*

Trying not to breathe too much, Kate silently gave her reflection one of Noah's pep talks: "You think it matters what they think? What they think don't matter! What matters is what's inside! What matters is Operation Defrost! Now get in there, and make the best of things!"

But when she and Mom got to the door of Room 29, she hesitated again. "Come *on,* honey," Mom said. She put her hand on Kate's shoulder, and before Kate knew it, she was standing inside the classroom. *Shoved by my own mother,* she thought.

"This must be Kate Sommers," said the teacher. "Mr. Payne told me all about you and your family." Kate looked at Mom. *What was that supposed to mean? How he practically broke his neck because of them?* But then the teacher winked. "Don't worry. I didn't believe a word."

Mom cracked up, and even Kate felt a little better. The teacher looked more like somebody's grandfather than like Dracula. He might be okay. As the room filled, he told them his name was Mr. Clouse. He'd been teaching for almost forty years, and if these sixth-graders didn't kill him, he planned to retire to Florida in June and "hang up my snow shovel forever."

Kate was aware that the kids walked in the door chatting, then got quieter. Are they whispering about me? she wondered. Mr. Clouse directed her to the coat rack. As she hung up her backpack and coat—red in a sea of blue and purple—she felt stares burning into her back. More whispers.

"Hey, what's *Iz-la Nay-da?*" a boy asked, reading Kate's sweatshirt.

When she turned around to answer, she seemed to be facing an audience. The sixth-grade class at Byrd Elementary didn't look so different from the kids in Isla Nada. They wore the same haircuts and similar clothes—except the boys' hats and jackets said Penn State and Steelers instead of USC and Rams.

I wish I was the kind of person who could say something funny, Kate thought. Then they'd like me. But instead she stammered, "I-It's where I live . . . Used to live. And we say it *Eye-la Nah-da.*"

"Well, ex*cu-u-use* me!" said the boy. He was tall and good-looking, with a Steelers sweatshirt. "I don't speak those foreign languages." Several kids laughed.

"Kate Sommers, Ryan Kuhn." Mr. Clouse nodded at

each. "Kate is from the Golden State. That's California, Ryan."

"Well, that's practically a foreign country," Ryan said. More laughter. Kate felt her cheeks burning and a twinge in her stomach. This was as bad as she had expected. She looked to her mom, but Mom was scanning the books on Mr. Clouse's desk.

Then the petite girl who had been smoking in the bathroom entered. The tobacco smell clung to her, and Kate wondered how she got away with it. Or maybe smoking wasn't a big deal here.

The girl grinned at Ryan, who gave her a too-cool nod back. I get it, Kate thought. Cutest girl, cutest guy. Kate had taken an instant dislike to stuck-up Ryan. They probably deserve each other, she thought.

"Tiffany Foster," Mr. Clouse said as the girl took her seat. "This is Kate Sommers. She'll be needing someone to show her around today."

Tiffany gave Kate a look that made Kate wonder if her nose needed wiping. But when Tiffany turned to answer Mr. Clouse, she smiled brightly. "Sure thing," she said.

Kiss-up, Kate thought.

Apparently Mom was suffering an acute attack of cluelessness, because she smiled at Tiffany and said—what could be more embarrassing?—"Take good care of her." Then she mouthed "Have fun!" to Kate and waved goodbye.

Kate wanted to run after her, like some scared kinder-gartner on the first day. But she settled for finding her seat and slouching down as small as possible. She was morti-fied when Mr. Clouse asked her to stand and say a few words about herself.

"Uh . . . I'm from southern California and we moved here because my dad's company closed their lawn mower factory and, uh . . . I have a little sister in first grade." Kate sounded like an idiot, and she sat down before anyone laughed at her again.

But Mr. Clouse wasn't finished. "I am afraid our chilly weather must come as quite a shock to you," he said. "Now, Kate, tell us, what hobbies do you enjoy?"

"Uh . . . do I have to stand up again?"

"As you like."

"I like to go in-lining—uh . . . that's like roller skating, kind of. And I collect seashells. And play volleyball. And I like to watch my boyfriend surf."

In the general murmur, Kate heard, "Oooooh—she's got a *boyfriend*," from a squeaky girl's voice, and, "You won't be doin' any *beach* stuff around here," from Ryan Kuhn.

Mr. Clouse shook his head. "Does anyone have any questions, *thoughtful* questions, for our new student?"

"Yeah." The girl sitting next to Tiffany raised her hand. She was also short, but square instead of petite.

Mr. Clouse called on her. "Madison?"

"Do you know any movie stars?"

Kate waited for everybody to laugh again, but they didn't. Could this girl be serious? "Uh . . . well, not exactly," she said, "but my mom was kind of in the business, and I have an uncle, his name's Tom Kooze, and—"

"Oooooh!" a girl squealed, "Can I meet him?"

"Can you get me his autograph?" another girl gushed.

Now everybody was talking, and Kate was confused. "I guess, but it's no big deal, he only makes used-car commercials . . . ," she explained, but they weren't listening anymore.

"*Class!*" Mr. Clouse raised his voice, and the room got quiet fast. "You will have many opportunities to speak with Kate Sommers today. Now, however, is your one and only opportunity to demonstrate your mastery of speed-writing. Get out pen and paper, please."

Speed-writing? What was that? Mr. Clouse leaned over Kate's desk. "It's something new we're experimenting with this year," he said. "You write for ten minutes on whatever topic comes to mind."

Weird, Kate thought, but she nodded.

"Is everyone ready?" Mr. Clouse looked at his watch. "Go!"

A lot of kids sat stunned like there wasn't a thought in their heads. But Kate didn't hesitate. *The Year My Parents Ruined My Life*, she wrote, then for ten minutes scribbled all that had happened since her dad had gotten the new job. She was describing a California bubble shell that Gramma had given her when Mr. Clouse called, "Time!"

Pouring out her heart that way made Kate feel better for a little while. But soon the feeling of confusion, that school was familiar but different, came back. The class discussed the Civil War, which Kate had studied in fifth grade. But she never heard of the novel they were reading. When they broke up into groups for math, Kate just sat there until Mr. Clouse remembered her. "Take a look at the book and tell me where you should be," he said. She recognized some stuff, but the pages seemed all out of order.

As lunch neared, Kate was terrified that Tiffany might forget her and terrified that she might not. Which would be worse: Sitting by herself while everybody stared and whispered? Or sitting with Tiffany, who would either ignore her or ask questions about movie stars she couldn't answer?

The lunch bell rang at 11:47, and by the time the second hand jerked to 11:48, the classroom was empty. Even Mr. Clouse was gone. And so was Tiffany.

No loss, Kate thought. I'll eat at my desk. She got her lunch from her backpack and pulled out a baggie full of crackers with weird green dots. Mom had borrowed a recipe from Mrs. Douglas. Kate's stomach churned, and she threw them back. The most normal thing she could find was an Oreo, and she had just swallowed it when

Tiffany appeared in the doorway. "I am totally *so sorry.*" Except her voice wasn't sorry. "I *forgot* all about you!"

There was a giggle, and Kate saw the square-shaped girl, Madison, behind her.

"Doesn't matter," Kate said. She didn't trust Tiffany a bit, and Madison seemed to be her shadow.

"You better get out of there," Tiffany said. "You will get in so much trouble if the hall monitor catches you. Don't you even know where the cafeteria is?"

"I thought you were supposed to show me," Kate said.

"Well don't pitch a hissy fit," Tiffany said. "I told you, I *forgot.*" Madison giggled again.

Kate didn't want to go with these awful girls, but even more she didn't want to get in trouble—especially if it meant a trip to see Mr. Payne. So she grabbed her lunch and followed Tiffany and Madison into the hall.

"The cafeteria's that way." Tiffany pointed vaguely toward the back of the school. "But we already ate, didn't we, Mad-One? Actually, I'm not that hungry. What I am is *dying* for a cigarette."

Kate thought that was an appropriate way to put it, but she didn't say anything.

"Me *too,*" Madison said.

Tiffany rolled her eyes. "You practically puke every time," she said. "But hurry up. They hardly ever check the primary kids' bathroom. Not that many first-graders smoke."

Madison laughed like this was hilarious.

Kate didn't want to hang out in the first-graders' bathroom while these two puffed away, but she followed them because she didn't know where else to go.

"So California must be so cool, and your uncle and your mom and everything," Tiffany said as they walked. "I guess Belletoona is like a big fat nowhere-burger to you, huh?"

"It's okay," Kate said. "I mean, it's not like it's some big deal to have an uncle in commercials."

"What uncle in commercials?" Madison asked.

"*My* uncle. Like I told everybody this morning."

Tiffany pushed on the bathroom door, which opened with a creak, looked inside, then motioned that it was safe. When the door closed, she pulled a pack of Virginia Slims out of her purse.

"Can I bum one off you?" Madison asked Tiffany. "Just till—"

"—just till forever. I oughta charge a buck apiece."

"*Pleee-ee-eeze*," Madison whined.

Tiffany ignored her. "Want one?" She tapped the pack so that a cigarette popped up and offered it to Kate.

"No thanks," Kate said.

"You chicken?"

Yeah, Kate thought. Too chicken to tell you what I think of you. But she just shrugged.

"Hey . . ." Tiffany was suspicious. "you won't fink, will you?"

"No!"

" 'Cause if you're one o' those kiss-up teacher-pet types . . ." Tiffany shot Kate a look, and for some reason Kate thought of the wild chimpanzees they had studied last year. Her teacher showed this video about a new one joining a troop, and they all got on each other, snarling and biting and scowling, until they figured out if the new one was supposed to be boss or not. Kate had thought chimpanzees were cute before that.

"Plee-ee-eeze, Tiffie, can't I have . . . ?" Madison was still whining.

"Oh, all *right*, Mad." Tiffany held the pack out, but at that moment the door creaked, and then it was wide open.

"Young ladies?" A tall woman with too-black hair and crow's feet stood in the doorway.

Smiling, Tiffany took charge. "Hi, Mrs. Ketchum. How are those second-graders? We were just down here reading to the kindergartners when Madison felt ill. Are you feeling better now, Madison?"

Tiffany was so smooth, Kate couldn't help being impressed. Madison wasn't as quick. "Ill?"

"You know, your stomach?" Kate, eyes searching for the pack of cigarettes, tried to clue her in.

Madison caught on abruptly, grabbed her middle and moaned such a loud fake moan that Mrs. Ketchum rolled her eyes. "You wouldn't want to let me have a look inside that purse of yours, Tiffany, would you?"

The open purse was slung over Tiffany's arm. She must have dropped the cigarettes in when she heard the door, Kate thought. Quick, but not quick enough. The Oreo flip-flopped in Kate's stomach. We're all gonna get it now.

"Oh gosh, Mrs. Ketchum. I mean, *sure.*" Tiffany's smile probably strained her cheek muscles. "There's just some books for the kindergartners in there, though. My favorite's *Pinocchio*, what's—?"

The bell interrupted her question. Instinctively Mrs. Ketchum looked at her watch, which was all the distraction Tiffany needed. "Oh gosh, we've *got* to get our stuff and get back to class!" Dragging Madison, she was through the door and down the hall before Mrs. Ketchum could stop her. "Have a good day!" Tiffany called back brightly.

Kate tried to get by, too, but Mrs. Ketchum wasn't going to lose all three of them. "And you are?" she asked.

"Kate Sommers. I'm new."

"Oh, yes. From California. Mr. Payne has told us all about you."

There was nothing to say to that. Kate held Mrs. Ketchum's gaze and waited. She couldn't get in trouble just for being in the restroom. Or could she? Everything was so strange and different here, maybe she could. Finally Mrs. Ketchum looked away, as if people bigger than second-graders made her nervous. "A word to the wise, Kate Sommers," she said. "Tiffany Foster has *always* been too smart for her own good."

Dad had insisted that Kate and Danielle walk home unless there was an actual blizzard. He said walking hadn't hurt him any as a boy, and it wouldn't hurt them either. So when the bell finally rang at three o'clock, Kate charged out of Room 29 and met Danielle at the flagpole.

Danielle babbled about how pretty her teacher was and how easy the reading was and how the girl next to her at lunch shared her pudding, and where was Kate anyway? She didn't see her in the cafeteria anywhere.

Kate didn't answer. She was thinking up a way to tell Mom she wasn't going back to that blurry school with those awful kids. She wished she was sixteen so she could get a job and earn the money for her airfare faster. Maybe if she offered to clean the house . . . ? Scrubbing toilets would be better than putting up with Tiffany Foster and her faithful shadow, the Mad-One.

But all Kate's arguments evaporated in surprise when she swung the front door open. The furnace ghost had graduated from *bang-bang-bang* to *BANG! BANG! BANG!* And Mom, wearing her parka, was up on a ladder in the dining room trying to rip down sheets of pink polka-dot wallpaper with her mittens on.

"Don't bother taking your coats off," she said instead of hello.

BANG! BANG! BANG!

"Is the furnace, uh . . . broken or something?" Kate asked.

BANG! BANG! BANG! the furnace answered.

"Not broken enough," Mom said.

"Is someone coming to fix it?" Kate asked.

Mom ripped off another sheet and climbed down the ladder to move it. "Your father said he'll take a look when he gets home."

"The house'll be an igloo by then!" Kate said.

Mom twisted around to face them. "*Look*," she said, "I have been on the phone to your dad three times today, and every time he insists the furnace is fine, that *I* must have done something to the thermostat." She turned back to the wallpaper and growled, "How was school?"

Kate and Danielle looked at each other. "Fine," they said in unison.

"Good."

BANG! BANG! BANG!

What with the furnace and the wallpaper and the fight when Dad got home, Mom forgot to tell Kate she had a letter until after dinner. By then Kate had lost the feeling in the tip of her nose and her earlobes, and even the dancing-ballerina-snowflake princess was immobilized — huddled in her bed under two blankets, her sleeping bag, and three beach towels.

Instead of eating dinner, Dad had taken a bag of Fritos to the basement. No one had seen him since, but now, in addition to *BANG! BANG! BANG!*, the walls said *plink-plink-plink* and *pom-papom-papom*.

Kate's heart had thumped when Mom finally remembered the letter. From Josh? But no; the return address was Molly's. Still, Kate was excited. Molly must be writing to say Operation Defrost was okay with her parents. For now the letter sat, unopened, on Kate's pillow. She wanted to get comfortable, warm even, so she could enjoy reading it. After all, it was the only good thing about the day, actually the only good thing since she got here.

She sat on the edge of her bed. Did it make sense to sleep in her snow boots? She settled for three pairs of wool socks, along with long underwear, her pajamas, an old sweater of her dad's, and her knit hat. Tucked in, her body wasn't cold, but she did wish she had a ski mask for her ears and nose.

Okay. Ready. She tore the envelope, pulled out the sheet of pink notebook paper, and read Molly's round, purple scrawl:

Dear Kate,   *Thanksgiving Day*

See, I told you I'd write, and you probably thought I'd forget, well I didn't. So ha-ha.

Today was boredom-ation because my whole family was here, even my cousins from San Berdu, and you know how well we get along. Not! So I go, "Let's go down to the walk," and they go, "It's too cold," and I go, "Let's listen to some tunes," and they go, "We'd rather watch Nickelodeon," and I go, "Okay," and so we sit around watching old TV shows like zombie-slugs, and Mom and Dad yell at us we should be doing something, and I'm all, "But I can't help it if they won't!"

After dinner they left, and Josh and Jessica and Justin and that new girl, Amanda, came over and we hung out until Daddy said he couldn't afford to feed an army. So now everybody's gone, and I have nothing to do so that's why I'm writing you.

I am keeping an eye on Josh like you said and I think he still loves you even though that girl, Amanda, is, like, so obviously hots-ation for him. It's not even funny.

I miss you! Especially yesterday when I went to Mag's Baggies and tried on suits and there was no one to tell me if I really looked fat. I bought one, but Daddy said I have to take it back because it's indecent, but he'll never see it. So ha-ha on him.

*I am not forgetting Operation Defrost, but I have
to bring it up at the right time. You understand, right,
chica? You know my parents.*

Your best friend,

Molly

P.S. — Have you seen any snow yet?

Kate read the letter over and over, each time thinking
she must have missed something. The third time she read
it her eyes filled with tears. "I *think* he still loves you"?
What was that supposed to mean? And that Amanda girl
was moving right in. Didn't Molly tell her to keep her
hands off?

But the worst part was that Molly didn't get it, didn't
realize how miserable and alone Kate was, how she was
absolutely one-hundred-percent counting on Operation
Defrost.

I'll call her, she thought, and picked up the phone.

"Kate?"

"Sorry, Mom." ·

She hung up. Things were worse than ever. Even her
mom was crying.

Chapter Eight

Weekend outlook; December 6 and 7, Belletoona, Pennsylvania: Cloudy, chance of snow.

"**B**ut there are icicles hanging from the ceiling!"

It was Friday afternoon, and Kate's mom was hollering into the telephone. The icicles were a lie, but Kate didn't blame her. If they went much longer without heat, the problem wouldn't be icicles, it would be more like murder.

"If five o'clock's the earliest . . . ," Mom took a tissue out of her pocket and wiped her nose. "Yes, I understand you'll have to charge extra." She hung up, sneezed into the tissue, then grinned.

"He's coming?" Kate said hopefully.

"He's coming!"

"Yesssssss!" Kate gave Mom a high five.

Up to now, Daddy wouldn't let Mom call a repairman because, he said, the furnace just needed a little more tinkering. He could do it himself. But this afternoon he finally gave in. That was after Mom had called and told him the water in the toilet bowls was frozen.

Unlike the icicles, this was true.

Instead of making dinner, Mom had spent the past hour dialing every number in the yellow pages under Furnace. With the freeze, they were all booked up. No wonder Mom was lying about icicles.

Kate was doing her homework at the kitchen table. Her system was to do math problems until she couldn't feel her fingers, then put on her mittens until she could, then take them off and do more math. It was slow, but it gave her time to go back and check. She was pretty sure she hadn't missed any.

Maybe I'll be one of the smart kids, she thought. Like I'm one of the quiet kids. That was the plan for making the best of the blurry school. It fit in well with being a nun. She would be so quiet, no one would notice her for the couple of months she was there. Then one day she would be gone, and no one would notice that either. Well, maybe Mr. Clouse would. After he read my essay

The Year My Parents Ruined My Life, he called her up to his desk and told her his parents made him move when he was a kid, and he didn't forgive them till he grew up.

"Maybe it won't take you quite that long," he said sympathetically. Then he gave her speed-writing an A.

Anyway, the quiet-kid plan wasn't as daring as Operation Defrost, but it had worked yesterday and today. Tiffany and her shadow had left her alone, even though sometimes she was sure they were whispering about her. At lunch, Kate sat at a table by herself, except for the Vietnamese girl in her class, Minh Duc. But Minh Duc hardly said anything; she probably didn't speak much English. So they just smiled at each other while Minh Duc ate rice and Kate ate crackers with green dots.

It was better than the first-grade bathroom.

Done with math, Kate put her mittens back on and blew into each to defrost her fingers. There was more homework yet. Mr. Clouse didn't care that it was Friday. That morning he had assigned a research paper in science, due in two weeks. "Think of something you really want to know about," he told them. "A mystery, if you will. Seek out the answer, and that's your paper."

A mystery? There was the phantom snowball. Could it really be a wild animal? It was an idea. Kate got a book about Pennsylvania wildlife out of the school library.

She was pulling the book out of her backpack when the doorbell rang.

"He's here!" Mom whooped.

Danielle, wrapped in her sleeping bag, stumbled to the door first. All three grinned expectantly as she pushed it open. But instead of the sight they longed to see—a grimy guy in coveralls—there stood Peter Douglas holding a cookie tin.

"Oh, it's you." Mom was so disappointed she forgot to be polite, just scowled and went back to the kitchen. Danielle heaved a big, dramatic sigh and followed. That left Kate and Peter staring at each other.

Kate felt bad. It wasn't Peter's fault he wasn't a furnace fixer. Not knowing what else to say, she invited him in. She expected him to say no. Who would want to go from one deep-freeze to another?

Peter Douglas, that's who. Through the door he walked, stuttering, "Uh . . . M-my mom made me . . . uh, I mean my mom told me I had to . . . uh, I mean . . . These are for you." He handed her the tin.

BANG! BANG! BANG!

"Thanks," Kate said.

Peter's eyes darted from walls to ceiling. "What was *that?*"

"What? Oh, *that?* Just the ghost."

"Really? Cool!"

He started to unzip his coat, but Kate shook her head. "I wouldn't do that."

"Oh, you want me to—?"

"No—you don't have to *go*. I just mean it's freezing in here. See, I have *my* coat on."

Peter nodded. "Can't miss *that* coat."

For a moment they just looked at each other. For the first time, though, she noticed that if he hadn't been so skinny and if his nose had been a little shorter, he'd be sort of cute. What does he think of me? she wondered.

Then she got a grip. Jeez, I must really miss Josh a *lot*.

Peter nodded at the tin. "Brownies."

"Thanks," Kate said again. Then a lightbulb flashed in her head. Peter's mom really was a great cook. The crackers from her recipe tasted like pizza. It turned out the green dots were oregano, not mold. "Would you like a brownie?" Kate asked him.

"*Yeah.*"

Kate was pointing Peter toward the kitchen when the doorbell rang again. Mom and Danielle flew by and all but hugged the man who stood on the porch.

"Where're them icicles?" he asked. "Never seen that before."

"Uh . . ." Mom thought fast. "I melted them. With a hair dryer. I was afraid they might pull down the ceiling. Sorry you missed it. This way." She pushed him down the hall.

Danielle tried to ask, "What icicles?" but Mom was louder. "Did I mention how *grateful* we are that you could come?" There were two entrances to the basement, one inside and one out. Mom showed him both, and together—with Danielle in tow—they clomped down to see the furnace.

Kate led Peter into the kitchen. "Mom keeps the oven on, so it's a little warmer back here." She explained about the bats in the fireplace while she opened the tin, which was totally stuffed with brownies, and put six on a plate. Then she got the milk. When she turned around, five brownies were gone.

"I saved you one," Peter said.

"You can eat it." The words were hardly out of her mouth before the brownie was in his. "Do you want some more?" she asked.

"If it's okay."

A few minutes later, Kate's dad came in the back door, home from work. "Door to the basement's open," he said, and kissed Kate.

"Mom's down there with the furnace guy."

"Ahhh." Dad nodded to Peter. "Nice to see *you*, young man!"

"Uh . . . yeah," Peter said.

"Do you have dinner plans?"

Uh-oh, Kate thought.

"Plans? Unh unh."

"Dine with us, then. Seems there's something in the

oven, and what did you bring in the tin? Smells like chocolate!" He turned to Kate. "Where's your mother, pip-squeak?"

"Basement with Dani and the furnace man. But Daddy . . . uh, can I talk to you for a minute?"

"Soon as I call young Peter's parents. Wouldn't want them to worry."

"Uh, *Daddy* . . ."

But he was already dialing.

Mr. Douglas must have answered, because Daddy brought up the furnace and the bats in the chimney—"I don't remember any mention of *those* when we signed the contract"—and answered a question about the broken snow shovel. He was laughing when he hung up.

"Your father's a card, Peter," Dad said. "He suggested we try a coal furnace, see if Flying Penguins do better shoveling 'the black stuff.' And he said he'd be delighted to have you on *my* grocery budget for dinner."

With the furnace guy working, new noises were echoing through the walls. Probably a good thing, Kate thought when Dad went downstairs to greet Mom. They will drown out the yelling.

Dad didn't stay in the basement long, and when he came up, he went straight to the pantry. "This enough?" He held up four cans of soup.

Kate looked at Peter, who was wiping brownie crumbs

off his chin. She shook her head: No way. Daddy held up five cans. Not enough. Six cans? Nope. Seven?

Finally, he opened all ten.

A few minutes later, the furnace guy left. He needed some parts to finish up, but what he'd done should hold for the weekend. Mom was so grateful, she planted a big kiss on his cheek. He walked out the door looking dazed, and he forgot to give them the bill.

By the time Dad served the soup, the house was warm enough that Kate could take her mittens off, and Danielle had traded her sleeping bag for a quilt. There had been one good thing about having a broken furnace, Kate thought. The cold had shut down the dancing-ballerina-snowflake princess.

During dinner, Peter said exactly seventeen words—Kate counted. He also ate bowl after bowl of soup: clam chowder, tomato, cream of broccoli, he loved them all. Mom must've felt bad about being rude earlier, because she was extra nice. "It's wonderful to feed someone who appreciates my cooking."

"Someone's cooking, anyway," Dad said. "Is there any more soup?"

"All gone." Mom shrugged.

"Just as well. I should save room for Mrs. Douglas's wonderful dessert." Dad got the tin from the counter and popped off the lid. "Hmm," he said, raising one eyebrow. "I suppose we could divide it five ways."

"Coldwell! Peter's our guest," Mom protested. "Here, dear, you take the last brownie."

"Thanks!"

Eighteen words.

Later, with Mom and Dad at the front door to say good-bye, Kate had a brainstorm. "Peter," she said, "would you say you're an average teenager?"

"Uh . . . sure," Peter said.

"Remember we talked about my coat?"

Peter nodded.

"Now tell the honest truth. Don't hold anything back. What do you think of it?"

He looked from face to face uncomfortably. "Dorky."

"Ha!" said Kate, and caught her father's eye. Peter was a pig, but he had come through in the clutch.

Chapter Nine

"You're tuned to WSNO, Belletoona, Pennsylvania, and this is meteorologist Bob Peary with a winter storm warning for Saturday, December six: Citizens are urged to stay off the roads due to unpredictable conditions throughout the . . ."

Mrs. Mooney clicked off the radio and smiled. "Nothing to worry about," she told Kate. "Those forecasters are a bunch o' nervous Nellies."

"Are you sure, dear?" Her husband was peering out the window. "Wind's picking up."

"I am *not* missing the Cashes' winter party on account of a breeze." Mrs. Mooney nodded at Kate. "It's *quite* the social event. Next year I'm sure your parents will be invited. I'll put in a good word."

She checked her lipstick in the hall mirror and adjusted the collar of her fur coat. Then she picked up Nicky Red-Suit, who was wearing red pajamas tonight, and handed him to Kate. He looked surprised but didn't protest. Maybe this will go okay, Kate thought hopefully.

Wrong.

As soon as the front door closed behind his parents, Nicky started to yell. Kate hauled him around the house, patting him and cooing. When that didn't work, she called home.

"Look in the medicine cabinet for cotton balls," her dad counseled.

Kate was too frazzled to ask why. With Nicky, still hollering, draped over one shoulder and the portable phone balanced against the other ear, she riffled through drawers in the downstairs bathroom. Finally she found a box of cotton balls. "Okay. Now what?" she asked.

"Take out two." Dad was talking loudly so that she could hear him over the baby. "And put one in each ear."

"His ears?"

"No! Yours! That's how I spent your entire babyhood. I don't think Danielle ever cried."

Kate threw the box of cotton balls down in disgust. "Let me talk to Mom!" she yelled.

Mom got right to the point. "Did you check his diaper?"

"No way!"

"Sooner or later, you have to," Mom said. "He's screaming anyway, so it might as well be now."

"Can't you come over and do it?" Kate begged.

"Honey, contrary to popular opinion, mothers don't like changing diapers any more than anybody else does. They especially don't like it when it requires trekking through a snowstorm first."

"Snowstorm?" Kate looked out the window. Sure enough, it was snowing hard. "Oh, all *right*," she said. "But if it's, you know, *messy*, I'm calling back."

Kate put it off as long as she could. She took Nicky to the window to show him the snow blowing in the gale. He screamed. She set him down and tried to teach him to play patty-cake. He screamed. She offered him every beverage in the refrigerator—from milk to diet iced tea. He screamed.

Finally she gave in, hauled him upstairs and laid him down on his changing table. This made him even madder, and he added kicks and punches to the noise. How was she ever going to do this? She tried to tune in to a pep talk, but she couldn't hear Noah's voice over Red-Suit's.

Then she had an idea: music. Didn't she read somewhere that it soothed savage beasts?

"Hush, little baby, don't say a word . . ." She began singing the first song she thought of. *"Mama's gonna buy you a mockingbird. . . ."*

"*Ma*ma! *Ma*ma!" Nicky howled.

This was the wrong choice.

"*Jingle bells, jingle bells, jingle all the way . . .* ," she tried again. "*Oh, what fun it is to ride in a one-horse open sleigh — hey!*"

Was she crazy, or was the crying a little softer? "*Jingle bells, jingle bells, jingle all the way. Oh, what fun it is to ride in a one-horse open sleigh — hey!*"

It was working! He wasn't kicking anymore, and the cries were more like gasps. She didn't think she better press her luck with the "Dashing through the snow" part, so she started over. "*Jingle bells, jingle bells, jingle all the way . . .*" Now he had settled down, but his face was red and tear-streaked, his nose runny, and his puffy, damp eyes mistrustful. Who says babies are cute? Kate wondered.

But she couldn't blame him for being mistrustful. She wouldn't want some incompetent stranger changing her diaper, either. Still singing, she untangled the pajamas from Nicky's chubby legs and then, reluctantly, the diaper from Nicky's bottom. *Oh yuck!* How could he do this to her?

For a moment, when she saw what she was up against, Kate stopped singing. But Nicky screwed up his face, ready to assault her ears like he was already assaulting her nose.

"*Jingle bells, jingle bells, jingle all the way . . .*" He relaxed again.

Kate reminded herself of Operation Defrost. This is earning me money for airfare, she said to herself. I have to do it.

Without breathing, almost without looking, she yanked off the old diaper and wadded it up. Then, holding Nicky by the ankles with one hand, she grabbed a soggy handful of baby wipes with the other and swiped at the disaster area. "*Oh what fun it is to ride . . .*" Nicky's breathing was steady now. I must've fooled him into thinking I know what I'm doing, Kate thought. "*. . . one-horse open sleigh—hey!*"

There. Clean. Well, clean enough.

Hastily, she stuck a fresh diaper on him and zipped his pajamas.

Then she breathed.

Twenty minutes later, after she had washed her hands and sung a zillion choruses of "Jingle Bells," Kate realized that Nicky's head felt heavy on her shoulder. Still singing, she carried him to a mirror so she could see his eyes. *Yes!* Closed!

In his room, she heard the wind outside moaning and the bump of a tree limb hitting the house. Oh, please, don't wake up, she thought as she maneuvered him into his crib. Under the covers, he sighed a long sigh. Kate just stood there. Nicky's tears had dried and his cheeks were rosy, not red. For a baby, she thought, he actually *is* kind of cute—when he's asleep.

As Kate crept out of Nicky's room, she was smiling. She had taken a screaming, smelly baby and transformed him into a quiet, sweet one. She didn't know she could do that. She wanted to call Molly and tell her, but she wasn't sure Molly would understand. And no way Josh would. Anyway, it was Saturday. Nobody would be home. In Isla Nada, she never stayed home on a Saturday night. Or baby-sat either. That was for kids with no social life — nuns like I am now, she thought.

Kate got a Coke and looked at the kitchen clock. It was 9:40 already. The Mooneys were supposed to be home before eleven, so she only had an hour to work on her paper. But eleven came and went, and Kate got so sleepy reading about snowshoe hares that she dozed off with her head on the book.

The phone woke her rudely. "Honey?" It was her mom. "Were you asleep? It's after midnight. Have Mr. and Mrs. Mooney called?"

"Hunh unh." Kate yawned. After midnight?

"I'm sure everything's fine," Mom said. "But give us a call if you get nervous."

When Kate hung up, she realized the storm had grown fiercer. Huddling on the sofa, she tried to read, but she couldn't concentrate. The windowpanes were clattering in the wind, then there was a crack that might have been a branch breaking. Where were the Mooneys anyway?

A few minutes later there was another crack and then a

bzzzz and then the lights went out. Kate was startled, relieved when they blinked on, terrified when darkness returned. Trying to get to a light switch, she bumped into the coffee table and bruised her shin. When finally she did flip the switch, nothing happened.

What do I do? she agonized. She had no idea where flashlights were. She made her way back to the sofa and sat down, put her head in her hands, tried to think. Her bruised shin throbbed. I'll call Mom and Dad! She felt for the phone, knocked the receiver to the floor, and had to feel for it again. Finally she caught hold and put it to her ear. No comforting hum. The phone was dead.

The storm, the lights, now the phone. It reminded her of every spooky movie she ever saw. And that's when a beam of light shone through the front window, danced around the living room, and caught Kate square in the eyes. When the doorknob rattled, she jumped so far her shin whacked the coffee table again. *Ow!*

"Ka-a-a-ate! Ka-a-*atie-e-e-e!*" a voice cried above the roar of the storm.

"Daddy?" She groped through the darkness again, cringing each time her shin touched something. Finally, hopping on one foot, she reached the door. When she opened it, the storm blew her dad inside and sent a flurry of snow with him.

"Not a fit night for man or beast," Dad said heartily, and Kate threw her arms around him—wet, snowy jacket and all. "Scared, pip-squeak? Nothing to worry about. Ice got the power lines is all. Think of the poor folks out on the poles."

Dad told her to take a nap on the couch, he would sit up and wait. But just as she was settling in—feeling safe and cozy with him beside her—she heard a noise from upstairs. Oh *no*.

"Sounds like we've got company," said Dad.

"Maybe he'll go back to sleep?" said Kate. But within sixty seconds, Nicky's screams were full blast, and Kate was using Dad's flashlight to make her way up the stairs. He's not going to like it when I'm not his mom, she thought. But when she got to his room, he held out his arms to her for rescue. She picked him up and he settled right in against her shoulder.

"Mama be home soon," she said.

"Jingah aw 'way," he answered, sniffling.

"What?"

"Jingah aw *'way!*" he insisted. What was he talking about? "Jingah aw *'way!*"

" 'Jingle Bells'? You want me to sing?"

"Sing," he commanded.

So Kate did, carrying Nicky in circles around his dark room. Twice she tried a different song, but both times he roused himself and demanded "Jingah."

It felt like it ought to be dawn, but it was only two when Kate heard the front door open and voices downstairs.

A minute later, Mrs. Mooney was in the room, apologizing, taking Nicky from her, apologizing again. The car got stuck, they had had to walk, finally a snow plow had given them a ride. And the party wasn't up to the Cashes' usual standards at all. Anyway, she was so *sorry*! If Kate would come around in the morning, she'd settle up.

"And don't worry," she added, yawning. "There'll be hardship pay."

"Jingah aw 'way!" Nicky was trying to get his mother's attention.

"What, sweetie?"

"I was singing to him," Kate explained. " 'Jingle Bells.' Now I guess it's your turn."

Chapter Ten

Long-range forecast for the Mid-Atlantic region: An onslaught of Arctic storms could produce record-breaking snowfall.

THE BELLETOONA *Bugle*, SATURDAY, DECEMBER 13

"Pennsylvania is part of the mid-Atlantic region," Danielle announced at breakfast. She was reading the newspaper again. Reading the newspaper was one way the total pest kissed up. No normal six-year-old cared about the stuff in newspapers. Normal six-year-olds cared about cartoons on TV and teddy bears and stick-on earrings.

Of course, normal six-year-olds didn't talk like they were forty and spend half their lives being the beautiful dancing-ballerina-snowflake princess either. Even before the house warmed all the way up, Danielle had wrapped the quilt around her waist and gone back to spinning and bumping into things.

Kate drank a sip of hot chocolate and tried to think if anything in her life had improved since last Saturday morning. The furnace worked again, there was that.

And Mrs. Mooney had paid her thirty-five dollars for her baby-sitting nightmare, besides asking her to sit again next week. With some birthday money Kate had saved, it was a good start on airfare.

What else? Well, Gramma had called the night before, and they had talked for a long time. Gramma always made Kate feel better, at least for a while. She wondered why old people, like Gramma and Mr. Clouse, understood so much more than regular grown-ups.

Kate took a bite—oh yeah, and there was breakfast. Mom had finally figured out how to make something that wasn't raw in the middle or lumpy: scones. Now the freezer was packed, and the family ate them almost every morning. Kate especially liked the ones with chocolate chips.

But scones might also be one reason Kate caught Mom crying on the bathroom scale yesterday. It turned out she had gained three pounds.

Okay, so there was heat, there was money, there was Gramma, and there was breakfast. But other than that, it was about as big a disaster as one little week could possibly be.

Danielle dabbed her mouth with her napkin, folded it, and put her hands in her lap. "May I be excused, Father?" she asked.

Kate rolled her eyes. "Oh give it *up*."

"*Kate!*" Dad gave her a warning look, then turned to Danielle, all sugar sweet. "Yes, dear, you may be excused. I appreciate a little civility. It has been in rather short supply of late."

"No lie," Kate muttered.

On Wednesday a fat letter had arrived from someplace called Moore, Payne & Sovereign, which turned out to be Mr. Payne's big lawyer relative. The letter was sitting on top of a stack of bills and credit card statements on Mom's desk. When no one was looking, Kate read it. Some words were as long as the ingredient names on snack bags, but Kate got the drift: Mr. Payne blamed her family for the crash that hurt his neck, and he wanted a whole bunch of money.

"That man's a pain in the neck," Dad had said at dinner. "Hey—that's a good one, eh? Mr. Payne-in-the-neck?" Nobody laughed.

There was more. At 3:27 Thursday morning, Kate heard another snap from across the street, and the next thing she knew the doorbell was ding-donging for dear life. When Daddy finally stumbled down the stairs and opened the front door, there stood Mr. Douglas with broken snow shovel number two.

Kate, Danielle, and Mom watched from the landing as Daddy explained that the Flying Penguin had been field-tested under extreme laboratory conditions, and therefore the problem must be improper technique. Considering he'd been woken up in the middle of the night, Daddy sounded very reasonable, Kate thought.

"You might benefit from one of our free snow-shoveling seminars, Douglas," Daddy said. "We serve complimentary coffee and doughnuts. The seminars are filling up quickly, but one word from me, and—"

When Mr. Douglas interrupted, he did not sound reasonable at all, and he used words Kate thought only teenagers knew. Mom covered Danielle's ears, but Dani kept trying to wriggle free. "What's he saying? What's that *mean*? Lemme *go!*"

Mr. Douglas must have heard her yelping, because he paused and then halfway apologized for losing his temper. Finally he calmed down enough to accept a couple of new shovels from the supply in the hall closet.

"Think about that seminar, Douglas!" Dad called as the door swung shut.

Great, Kate thought. Now we're at war with the principal and at war with the neighbor. Pretty impressive for living here only two weeks. But compared to the real problem, this stuff was just annoying. The real problem was Byrd Elementary School, specifically the kids at Byrd Elementary School. She had told Gramma all about it on the phone the night before. But she couldn't bother her parents—they had their own stuff to worry about. And she could never get hold of Molly. Either Mom was tying up the phone, or Molly was grounded and couldn't talk, or her line was busy. Finally, on Friday, Molly was there and allowed to talk, but somebody came to the door practically before Kate said hi.

"Just a sec!" Molly yelled. "Ooh, *chica*, I gotta go! I'll call ya right back, 'kay?"

"Who is it?" I'm her best friend, Kate thought. Who could be more important?

"Uh . . . some guy. I'll call ya back."

"Some guy?" And she didn't call back, either. Anyway, since the phone hadn't gotten her anywhere, Kate was planning to write Molly a long letter after breakfast. She thought of chewing her out for being rude, but probably she better not. She was counting on Molly to convince her parents, after all.

Kate did not ask to be excused, just cleared her plate and put it in the dishwasher. She was on her way to the stairs when Danielle spun into her. "What *is* it with you, anyway?" Kate snapped.

"I'm the beautiful dancing—"

"Demented-ballerina-snowflake *retardo* is more like it."

"At least I don't have hal-luc-i-mations!" Concentrating on the long word, Danielle bumped into a wall, bounced off, and went the other way.

"Halluci-*what?*" Kate followed her into the living room.

"That snowball phantom thingy. Nobody else sees it. It's your hallucination." Danielle spun around the couch.

"It's pronounced hal-lu-ci-*nation*, pest," Kate said. "And anyway, how do you even *know* that word?"

"That book Mom gave me." Danielle spun across the hall and into the dining room, where the furniture was covered with sheets because Mom was getting ready to paint. "There were lots of new words in that book." Danielle bumped into a ladder. "The pirates eat this stuff and they have hallucimations. Not snowballs though. Sea monsters and mermaids."

"Well, for your information, the phantom snowball is real," Kate said.

She left Danielle spinning through a paint-bucket obstacle course. In her room, Kate got Gramma's stationery from her desk, curled up on her bed, and wrote:

Dear Molly,
   How are you?
   I am so awful I don't know where to start. With Tiffany and the Mad-One, I guess, because they are the worst.
   Or I could tell you how Ryan Kuhn, that's Tiffany's boyfriend, cornered me and put his hand on my shoulder and told me my hair's pretty — like he thinks he's

God's gift to womanhood—and I had to practically sock him to get him to leave me alone. At least I pushed him hard. He acted like a wounded puppy, and now he doesn't even look at me, which is the only good thing that has happened since I started school.

I wanted to tell Mr. Clouse—he's my teacher—but all I need is a snitch reputation, right? So I didn't say anything.

Anyway, back to Tiffany, who is president of the sixth-grade class, and also cute, and also gets good grades, which is hard to believe because she is dumb enough to smoke. Anyway, Tiffany has hated me since the first day I got here, which I can't figure out, and she's really mean about it, too.

You know how I have that old red coat? Well, no one has to tell me what it looks like because I know and I've been begging for a new one. So before school I was hanging it up and behind me there's this giggling and whispering. It's Tiffany and her shadow, this fat girl Madison:

"Maybe everybody in California has a big ugly red coat."

"Yeah, like in Hollywood."

"Yeah, like Tom Cruise."

"Except even a big ugly red coat would look good on Tom Cruise."

"*Definitely! But not on a girl. It would just make a girl look even taller and more stuck-up than she already is.*"

You get how sweet Tiffany and the Mad-One are? Plus there's this whole Tom Cruise thing, which is so weird. The kids here act like we're friends or something. Do they really think everybody in California hangs out with movie stars? (Not that I'd mind!!!)

So all this happened on Monday and Tuesday, then, if you can believe it, things got worse. First I have to explain how it's different here than in Isla Nada. There all our friends are sort of ordinary, like they come from ordinary families like yours and mine. I mean, lots of kids' parents are divorced, but besides that we mostly have houses that are alike and parents who have credit cards for the mall and there are snacks in the kitchens, right?

So here it's not like that. Our house is old, but it's nicer than a lot of people's and it's a big deal that my dad manages a factory. In my class, some kids' parents don't have jobs and some kids' dads work for my dad at the factory. Then there are doctors' kids, too, like the Mad-One's mom is a doctor, so she's one of the "rich" kids and so am I. Isn't that weird? I mean, I don't think I'm rich. (Anyway, I'm totally not rich enough to get a new coat!!!)

So there is this one girl here, Minh Duc, and she's Vietnamese. I don't think she speaks much English, but she smiles a lot so I like her. I mean, I have to like somebody. We sit at lunch together and don't talk. So Wednesday she forgot her lunch and her mom couldn't bring it, and I felt bad so I was going to lend her money for the cafeteria, and when I opened my wallet this snoopy girl, Ashley, saw I had a 20 in there (from baby-sitting) and the next thing I know everybody's asking to borrow money like I'm some kind of bank.

Only it's not like they really want money, it's just they want to make fun of me for being "rich," you know?

So now I can't go to school without somebody saying, "Hey, California! (That's what they call me.) Can I borrow lunch money, too?"

And Minh Duc was totally embarrassed. I guess she speaks enough English to get the drift. And I felt just as bad for her as I did for me. Worse.

You can imagine by Friday I was never going back to school, only things aren't that good for my mom either, and all she needs is for me to throw a tantrum. So Friday morning I was in the restroom psyching myself up to go to class when Tiffany came in to smoke. I mean, I'm like sitting in the restroom, crying my brains out, and I hear somebody, and then I smell the stink and I know it's her. Well no way am I going to let her see me so I just stay in the stall for practically ever until finally I hear her leaving.

That's when the lights go out! I mean, it sounds like big deal, the lights go out, but all of a sudden it's totally black, and I'm thinking a fire burned up the electricity and I'm trapped in the restroom! (Sometimes I am as bad as Dani.) I am not kidding, Molly, I was terrified. It was only when I got it together enough to unlock the door to the stall (in the dark!) and bump along to the hall door that I realized the switch was turned off, and Tiffany did it!!!

By then, of course, I'm late and I think I should just cut, but where would I go? It's snowing (like always) outside, and I don't want to freeze. So I walk into class and Mr. Clouse is all, "Where were you, young lady . . . ?" until he gets a look at the way my eyes are all red and my face is all blotchy and then he's all, "Honey, what's the matter?" and he makes me come up to his desk and talk to him, and I hear them all whispering and giggling.

Mr. Clouse is nice, but what can he do about anything? He's just a teacher.

So at lunch I'm sitting with Minh Duc, and Tiffany comes up with Madison—they are joined at the hip—and she says, "Oh, Kate, I'm so totally sorry. Were you in the restroom when I turned the light out?

I was just trying to save electricity. Did it scare you? Is that why you were crying?"

And all the time Madison's giggling like the puff-brain she is.

So I just eat my scone, and later I hear Tiffany telling Ashley how I'm so stuck-up I won't talk to her.

I better stop writing because my hand is cramped up which I'm sure you can believe because by now your eyeballs are probably sore!!! This is the longest letter I ever wrote, but I just have to talk to you, you know? And I can't get you on the phone. I was sort of mad yesterday when you hung up, but that's okay. Who was the guy? Is he gorgeous?

Please, Molly, talk to your parents right away! If I thought I had to stay here, I would die.

Your (desperate) best friend always,

Kate

Kate put the pen down and shook her hand to get rid of the cramp. Usually she read letters over in case she spelled something wrong, but this time she didn't. It was sad enough the first time.

By now, Kate knew the mail schedule. If she got her letter into the box on the corner before one, it would go out that day. She was fastening her snow boots when she heard some kind of ruckus in the dining room: Danielle's shrill howl, followed by Mom yelling, then Dad with the low notes. What now? Letter in hand, Kate hurried down the stairs. As she got closer, she could make out what was being said.

"I didn't mean to!" That was Danielle. "Meaning to isn't the point!" Mom sounded tearful. "Can we just settle down a minute here?" As usual, Dad tried to make peace. "Will somebody please get a rag?" Mom again.

Kate wasn't even halfway down when she saw the pool of evidence at the bottom of the stairs. So that's what happened, she thought. She tiptoed over the fingers of paint stretching across the wood floor and looked around the corner into the dining room. Two buckets were knocked over, Mom was still yelling, Dad was on the floor with a rag, and Danielle looked miserable.

Kate knew it was mean, knew she would be roped into helping clean up, but she couldn't help it: *Yesss!* she thought. Dancing-ballerina-snowflake princess bites the dust!

Chapter Eleven

Christmas Day, Belletoona, Pennsylvania: Snow, clearing by nightfall.

"Isn't this glorious?" said Dad as he came down the stairs Christmas morning. "A white Christmas!" He burst into song.

"Daddy, *please!*" Kate and Danielle protested. His singing was one thing they agreed on.

"Angela, these children don't appreciate good music," Daddy complained.

"I think they're eager to get to the presents, dear. And *I* want to see how the Christmas bread turned out."

It was snowing, which was no big surprise. It never stopped snowing. The drifts in the yard were so high you couldn't see the street from the house. The small trees had disappeared, and even the tallest ones looked shrunken. On the phone to Gramma, Mom called the snowbanks piled by the curb the Great Walls of Belletoona.

With all the shoveling practice she got, Kate had learned to arc her upswing just right. She was getting muscles, too. She couldn't wait for beach volleyball this spring to show them off.

Kate was in a good mood. It was Christmas, after all, and there were presents to look forward to—including one from Josh. Also, she had been out of school for five days and didn't have to go back for another week. It was a lot more fun to shop, wrap presents and bake scones with Mom than it was to face Tiffany and the Mad-One day after day.

But best of all was Molly's Christmas card, which had arrived yesterday:

Dear Kate,   *Dec.* 20

  Thank you for all the letters. I am so surprised you hate it there. Ha-ha. Just kidding.

  I talked to my parents about Operation Defrost. My mom says it is okay if you stay here if you still want to by the time you earn the airfare. But she says I have to give away my stuffed animals so your clothes will fit in the closet. I think she is kidding about that last part.

I am still bugging my dad. First he said no because he is not feeding any more teenagers. But don't worry because Mom is on my side, and I will never stop bugging him, and he always gives in when "the women gang up on him." That's how he says it.

It is really hot here and I ran out of sunscreen and now my nose is red and I'm so scared I'm going to peel. I put gobs of papaya moisturizer on it and then I went and lay down on my bed with a wet peppermint tea bag on it like a mask, you know? But I still look like Rudolph, which I guess is appropriate for Christmas. Ha-ha.

Mandy is here and we are going to the mall. You remember Mandy? She finally stopped wearing those hippie-dippy clothes and now we get along good. She says she thinks Josh is so immature, which I don't, but everybody is entitled to their opinion, right?

So bye.

Your best friend,

Molly

Kate had put the card in her desk drawer so her parents wouldn't see it. She wasn't ready to tell them about Operation Defrost yet. She wished Molly's dad had said plain yes. And she wished Molly had said Mandy was keeping her hands off Josh. (Thinking he was immature didn't prove anything, did it?) Not to mention how it was too bad Molly treated everything like a big joke. Ha-ha.

But that was Molly's way, and besides, how could she understand, really understand, what Kate was going through? To her a big crisis was if your nose peeled. Did I used to be like that? Kate wondered.

"Come on, everybody!" Danielle was impatient. "Father, you sit over there, and Mother, you're on the sofa. Katie can have the floor."

Kate surveyed the loot under the enormous tree. Mom's relatives were all in California, and Dad's had left Buffalo for Florida a long time ago. None of them wanted a thing to do with snow, so instead of coming to visit, they had sent a fleet of delivery trucks. Package after package had been left on the front porch.

Santa had come through too, even in a snowstorm. Both Danielle's and Kate's stockings—hung by the chimney with care—were stuffed.

Danielle was looking at the stockings, too. "How do the reindeer fly when it's snowing?" she asked.

"They live at the North Pole, silly," said Kate. "They're used to it."

Danielle looked at Mom. "Tell the truth. Did *you* fill our stockings?"

"Are you kidding?" Mom asked. "You think I'd go Christmas shopping in the *snow*?"

"True," said Danielle. "I guess magic *is* the most likely explanation."

"Are you sure you don't want breakfast first?" Daddy was teasing.

"*Presents!*" Kate and Danielle answered together.

"Good," said Mom. "I don't think the bread's done yet."

Danielle got a package from under the tree. "I'll be Santa!" she declared.

The unwrapping began. Kate liked the first two sweaters. But after the muffler, the hat, two pairs of mittens and a third sweater, her "Oh, wow, neat," was not so convincing. The only thing she smiled about, really smiled about, was a hundred-dollar check from Gramma. The ads in the paper said airfare to Los Angeles was $350. With her baby-sitting savings, she was more than halfway there.

As Kate watched Danielle tear the plastic off her new Snowflake Barbie, she remembered last Christmas. Santa had given her in-line skates, the ones she had left in Isla Nada with Molly. And there had been a Boogie board, too, and a bathing suit, magenta bike shorts, a Frisbee, and a Minnie Mouse visor. After the presents were done, she had gone down to the walk to try the skates. She remembered the thrill of gliding fast, then faster—and the hospital, of course.

After Molly laughed at the "dorky-looking" wrist pads,

Kate had taken them off. She was zooming downhill when she had to dodge an old lady walking a sheepdog. That's when she hit the soda can and went airborne. Molly said it was awesome, until the crash landing. Dad took one look at Kate's right arm and drove her to the emergency room for X rays. But nothing was broken, the doctor gave her a candy cane, and she even got home in time for dinner.

Kate sighed. She would never have that good a Christmas again.

"This one's for Kate." Danielle handed her a small box. On the wrapping paper were Santas on surfboards.

At last!

"What does the card say?" Daddy asked.

Kate read it aloud. "This was sure hard to find! From, Josh." Kate had already read it, of course, and she had shaken the package and held it up to the light and slept two nights with it under her pillow. She hadn't peeked, though. That would be cheating.

To Josh she had sent a new leash for his board—even though it had meant dipping into her baby-sitting money. There were no surf shops in all Pennsylvania, so she mail-ordered from a company in *Teen Surf*. It was a really cool leash, with a urethane cord and a quick-release rail saver. Of course she wrote him a mushy card and signed it "Love," but she had told herself not to be disappointed about his card signed "From." He probably knew she would read it in front of her family. Guys get embarrassed easy.

Kate turned the package over one more time, enjoying the suspense. Sunglasses maybe—from that store at the mall she and Molly loved? Or earrings—tiny surfers to wear to the Valentine dance?

"Oh, give it *up*, Katie!" Danielle was exasperated.

Kate laughed and ripped the paper, trying to contain her excitement. Then she lifted the lid off the box, removed layers of tissue paper and . . . *oh, heartbreak!* Out came a pair of red-and-green wool socks with reindeer leaping around the toes.

There was a moment of silence, exactly like a funeral, then Mom chirped, "Well, wasn't that *thoughtful!*" and Danielle added, "Not very sexy."

"And where," Dad looked at Danielle, "did you hear that word?"

"This book Mom gave me to read on the plane," she answered. "The pirate was sexy. His girlfriend was sexy. Practically *everybody* was—"

"That's enough for now, Dani," said Mom.

"What book—" Daddy began, but Mom silenced him by nodding at Kate. She had put her head in her hands and was sniffing back tears. The socks had been tossed on top of the crumpled gift wrap.

"Oh, honey, don't cry." Mom came over and hugged

her. "I remember one year your dad gave me flannel pajamas for Valentine's Day—"

"They were *red*!" Daddy protested.

"Coldwell. Get a clue. We were newlyweds, and it was Valentine's Day!"

Danielle chimed in. "Yeah, Daddy, she wanted something sexy!"

"You stay out of this." Daddy glowered, and Danielle closed her mouth.

Kate was snuffling against Mom's shoulder. She was totally embarrassed to be such a baby on Christmas, and she totally couldn't help it. What was that supposed to mean, a pair of socks?

"There are still presents to open, honey," Mom said kindly.

"I dow." Kate sniffled.

"He probably sent socks because he got a new girlfriend," Danielle said.

"*Dani!*" Mom and Dad both tried to shush her.

"I never liked him. All he is is pretty. I like Peter across the street. He has friendly eyes, even if he did eat all our brownies."

Kate wanted to pound the total pest for being so dumb. How could anybody compare Josh to Peter Douglas? They were from different *planets*.

Kate rubbed her eyes and got up. "Excuse be a biddit." In the bathroom she blew her nose. Christmas is ruined.

Christmas is ruined. Christmas is ruined. Christmas is . . .

Oh, give it *up*, Kate! She needed one of Noah's half-time speeches: "What're you gonna do, let that old sock-giver ruin your Christmas?"

When Kate came back to the living room, everybody looked up hopefully, and she smiled. "I'b okay." When she sniffled, her head cleared. "I'm really okay. Here, Dani, let me play Santa." She retrieved her gift for Mom, wrapped in palm-tree paper. It was a video, and Mom laughed and held it up: "*How to Stuff a Wild Bikini!*" she read. "Should we have a beach party?"

"Do you think it's appropriate for family viewing?" Dad studied the box.

"Don't worry," Danielle said, "I already know all about *sexy*."

Daddy opened his mouth, closed it, then opened it again. Finally he said, "What say we take a break from presents? I'm hungry!"

"Oh no!" Mom jumped up. "My *bread!*"

The table in the dining room was pretty: poinsettia centerpiece, Christmas-tree china, goblets for the orange juice. And yellow paint was a big improvement over pink polka dots. You had to look hard to see the spatters they missed after the dancing-ballerina-snowflake princess's finale.

"Angela? Do you need anything in there?" Dad called into the kitchen when everyone else was seated.

There was no answer.

"Uh-oh," said Danielle.

A minute later Mom came in. She was carrying the silver platter, which she placed in front of Daddy. In its center was something that resembled a mud brick with icing.

"Mmm," said Dad. "Looks wonderful, sweetheart."

"Yeah," Mom said, "if you're building a house."

"Now, don't be hasty, Angela. Let's give it the old college try," Dad said. He took the bread knife and began sawing. Nothing happened. He smiled at Mom, got a firmer grip, and tried again. This time the force of the knife flipped the brick into the air, and it bounced end over end across the wood floor. When it came to rest, everyone looked at it until Dad broke the silence. "I have an idea. Angela, you sit here and enjoy your hot chocolate."

"You mean I've done enough damage?"

Dad patted her shoulder, left the brick where it lay, and went into the kitchen. Soon they heard crinkling paper and clinking dishes. Whatever he was doing took a long time.

When he came back, he was carrying four cut-glass dessert bowls and a silver pitcher on a tray. "Madame?" He placed a bowl in front of Mom. "Ma'm'selle?" He gave bowls to Kate and Dani. "Monsieur?" He put a bowl at his own place, then set the pitcher in the center of the table.

Danielle couldn't believe it. "Froot Loops?"

Dad raised an eyebrow. "Froot Loops, *oui*," he said in a fake accent. "But zey are not ze Froot Loops *ordinaire*. Zey are ze Merry Christmas Froot Loops."

Mom looked into the bowl quizzically, took a bite, looked into the bowl again and burst out laughing. She laughed so hard she sprayed Froot Loop bits all over the poinsettia. "Look," she said. "There are only red and green ones! Daddy separated out all the others."

After breakfast, Dad insisted on shoveling before they opened the remaining presents. "Otherwise," he did his Mr. Douglas imitation, "ya got ice to contend with!"

Kate threw on her winter layers, grabbed a shovel from the closet, and joined her dad on the front steps. She was never exactly clear about what happened next.

Daddy said something about how beautiful the icicles were, she remembered that, and Kate looked up and . . . the next thing she knew she was lying on stiff sheets under bright lights, and half her face felt numb.

"Lucky really, the poor kid," said a woman's voice. "Half an inch, and it would've meant an eye. You'd be surprised how much damage icicles do. Why, just yesterday—Oh, look. She's back. Katherine? How do you feel?"

Kate blinked, but it hurt and she closed her eyes again. "What happened? Where—?"

"Emergency room," said the woman.

"Second Christmas in a row," she heard her dad say.

"Daddy?" Kate tried to blink again. There was some kind of stuff stuck to her eyebrow.

"Right here, pip-squeak. It's all my fault. I should have realized the ice was melting. I—"

"Don't blame yourself, Coldwell."

"Mom?" Kate wanted to look around, but her head was too heavy.

"Icicle fell smack on your face," said the woman's voice. "You were pretty woozy, but your vitals were fine so I stitched you up. The scar shouldn't be bad, though. I'm a fair seamstress. Now,"—she held up three fingers— "how many fingers? Or are you any good at math?"

The doctor turned out to be Madison's mom— wouldn't you know it?—and she thought Kate should stay a night in the hospital. Mom and Dad and the total pest spent all afternoon with her. Mom wanted to cancel dinner at the Douglas's, but Kate insisted they go. They hadn't eaten anything all day except Froot Loops, and she didn't mind watching TV.

It was almost time for them to leave when Mom put a big square box marked "With love from Santa" on the bed. "Last one," she said.

A volleyball? No, too flat. Snow boots maybe. But when Kate lifted the box, it seemed too heavy. Without much hope, she tore the paper and looked inside. At first they looked like in-line skates, incredibly ugly in-line skates, plain white leather and white laces. But then she pulled them out and saw blades where the wheels were supposed to be.

Her parents were grinning. Kate tried to smile back, but it made her face hurt. The numbness was wearing off. "Ice skates," she said. "Oh, wow, neat."

"When I was a boy in Buffalo—" Dad began.

"It's a lot like in-line skating." Mom ignored him. "I even asked Peter Douglas about it. The kids go to that pond in the town square . . ."

"They're really nice," Kate said. "Thanks." It was the best she could do. She hoped it sounded at least halfway sincere. Her parents had tried.

"I thought Santa gave her that present," Danielle said. "How come she's thanking you?"

"If Santa were here, I'd be thanking him." Kate was surprised her brain still worked this fast. "But he's not, so I'm thanking them."

"Oh," said Danielle, thinking. "But—"

"Dear me, we're late," Daddy interrupted. "We'll be back after dinner, bring you some tidbits, pip-squeak."

Danielle was still trying to ask about Santa as they walked out the door. Kate closed her eyes. She thought of calling Molly or Gramma, but her face hurt so much she didn't want to hold the phone to her ear. Oh, misery, she thought, and a tear rolled down her cheek. Somewhere in the back of her mind the voice of Noah tried to get a word in.

Shut up, Kate thought.

Chapter Twelve

Study documents mid-winter 'blahs'
Says thousands suffer unfocused rage, depression
THE BELLETOONA *Bugle*, WEDNESDAY, JANUARY 14

"What's *unfocused rage?*" Danielle asked. She was reading the paper at breakfast again. She does it to drive me crazy, Kate thought. It's almost as bad as the dancing-ballerina-snowflake princess, except so far not as dangerous.

Mom looked to see what Danielle was reading. "When you're mad at something but you don't know what," she explained.

"You mean like when you threw your new radio out the window?"

"Exactly." Mom went back to rinsing Froot Loop scum

from the cereal bowls. "Hurry up and eat. It's almost time for school, and I want to be at the mall when it opens."

The radio, small enough to fit in a pocket, had been a Christmas gift from Dad. The tag said, "To keep you company around the house." Mom had laughed and even given him a kiss. But that Saturday afternoon, she pitched a fit like Kate couldn't believe. It started when she and Dad had an argument about a second letter from Mr. Payne's lawyer. Dad claimed they didn't have to worry because he heard Mr. Payne was in trouble with the school board anyway. Mom said what did that have to do with anything?

After, Mom had called Gramma, but Gramma wasn't home. Then she went to the market and there were no avocados for guacamole. Plus, she said, she spent twenty minutes looking for tortillas and finally found them next to the yogurt—the yogurt!—and they had never even heard of whole wheat.

She lost it entirely when Daddy said he liked how her new jeans fit.

"They *aren't* new jeans," Mom snapped. "They're the same *old* jeans only they're so tight now I can hardly squeeze into them." Next thing Kate knew—*crack!*—through the window went the radio. "I never *wanted* a radio!" she had sobbed while she swept up glass. "What I want is a life!"

Kate thought of inviting her along on Operation Defrost. But of course Mom couldn't leave Danielle and Dad, no matter how miserable she was. And today she was back to making the best of things—going to the mall to buy herself jeans "to fit an elephant" and a new radio. She offered Kate a coat, too, but Kate said it was okay.

I won't need a coat in California, she thought. She still hadn't found a way to tell her parents she was leaving, but she would have to soon.

Molly had called Christmas Day—they must have been at the hospital—and Daddy saved the message on the answering machine:

"Is that the long beep or—Oh, I guess it was.

"Hi, Mr. Sommers. This is Molly Blossom. In Isla Nada? I'm not interested in a snow-shoveling seminar (giggle) because all we have is sand (giggle), even though I like doughnuts and everything—especially, you know, with sprinkles.

"So . . . anyway . . . uh, I'm just calling to say Merry Christmas, Kate, and don't worry about anything because it's all gonna work out fine, *if you know what I mean* (giggle).

"And thanks for the penguin charm for my bracelet, which I thought was so cute and funny. And I'm sorry I didn't send you anything but I do have this thing for you and I didn't want to mail it because I'll be seeing you soon anyway, I mean uh . . . not *that* soon, if your parents are listening, and anyway, I gotta go. Bye."

It was just like Molly to slip that way, but nobody asked about it. Probably her parents didn't even listen to the whole message. Kate tried to call her right back, but almost a week went by before she reached her. She told her about the icicle and the socks Josh sent, and was he seeing that Amanda girl or what?

Molly wanted to know how ugly the scar was and said Josh definitely wasn't seeing Mandy, who anyway was really nice. "When you get here you'll see. We hang out together now."

And had Molly convinced her dad?

"You worry too much, *chica*! It's all set. Mostly. I'll even meet you at the airport."

Kate felt better. And when Josh checked in to say happy new year, she felt way better. True, he never said flat out he loved her, but that wasn't his style. And when she hinted that maybe socks weren't the most romantic present, he got crabby. "We went to *three* stores!" She forgot to ask who "we" was but figured out later it must have been he and his mom.

The important thing was that he called at all and said sure he'd go to the dance with her if she was there. Ease up a little, wouldja? He had promised, hadn't he?

"Well, I'll be there," Kate told him. She had baby-sat Red-Suit a couple of times over vacation—she was the first baby-sitter he really liked, according to Mrs. Mooney—and now she had almost enough for the ticket.

She thought about taking back the ice skates, which must be worth a hundred dollars at least, but she couldn't hurt Mom's and Dad's feelings like that. They had looked so hopeful when they had given her the box. Anyway, there was a month till the Valentine's dance, enough time to earn the rest and talk to her parents. She just had to put up with blurry Byrd Elementary School, Tiffany, and the Mad-One, and Ryan, and Ashley the snoop, and Mr. Payne, and the entire sixth grade, for a little while longer.

At school that morning, Mr. Clouse made an announcement. "If the weather doesn't worsen, Mr. Payne has approved a little surprise for you later. You might keep that in mind as you comport yourselves."

By now, Kate was used to Mr. Clouse's way of talking. He was telling them to behave or they wouldn't get their treat, whatever their treat was. It was weird, but Mr. Clouse was the main thing Kate would miss about Belletoona. In Isla Nada, school had been something to put up with between episodes of real life, which took place at the mall, at the beach, on the walk, and in the family rooms of her friends' houses.

Here, real life meant school, homework, baking scones with Mom, and baby-sitting. Mr. Clouse made class interesting. Kate had been proud of the A+ she got on the phantom snowball paper. She had worked really hard on it and learned a lot about white-tailed weasels, but the mystery remained unsolved. Come to think of it, she hadn't seen the snowball for a while. She hoped it was okay, whatever it was.

After lunch, Mr. Clouse announced the surprise. Instead of PE in the gym, the class was going sledding on the hill behind the school. "All *right!*" Ryan Kuhn shouted, and there were claps and whistles. Only Kate despaired. Her dad had gone sledding with Danielle, but so far Kate had always managed to get out of it. It was a nasty trick to get trapped into it at school.

Still zipping and tying, Kate trailed out behind the rest of the class. They were whooping it up—couldn't wait to get to the top of the hill. What was the matter with these kids? Why would anybody want to thump, bump and bruise their way down a slope with only a thin sheet of plastic between their bottom and frozen-ation?

She caught up with Minh Duc, who didn't look too excited about sledding either. They smiled at each other, then Minh Duc reached into her pockets and came up with a pair of mittens. "I have extra," she said. "You could put them on over your gloves."

Her English is getting better, Kate thought. She wiggled her fingers to see if they were numb. Not yet. "That's okay, Minh. Thanks, though."

"I don't like sledding," Minh Duc told her. "When I was little, I hit a tree and got banged up."

Kate knew Minh Duc spoke some English and understood things, but that was a pretty long sentence. Minh sounded like, well—an *American*. "Minh Duc, can I ask you something?"

"Sure."

"Did you take English lessons over break?"

"English lessons? Do I need them?"

Kate's jaw dropped. "You mean . . . all this time? You speak regular English?" Then she realized that might sound insulting, and the last thing she wanted was to insult the only nice kid in the entire town. "I didn't mean, I mean—I *know* lots of Vietnamese people speak—I mean, I shouldn't have assumed just because—"

Minh Duc smiled, thank goodness. "You thought because I don't say much I didn't speak English? That's funny, Kate. I was born here. I'm just shy. Like you."

By now, they were standing at the top of the hill, waiting for Ron and Sam, the boys Mr. Clouse had sent to get the sleds. Kate was stamping her feet to keep warm. An occasional snowflake floated down; one melted on her nose. I'm not shy, Kate thought. No surprise Minh Duc thinks so, though. That had been the plan, hadn't it? Be so quiet no one would pay attention to me. But maybe it kept me from making a friend, too.

Kate looked down the hill, which was a lot steeper from the top than from the bottom. "I never did this before," she admitted.

"Sit down, hold on, close your eyes," said Minh Duc.

Kate nodded. And then you run into a tree, she thought—no wonder. She was watching the boys drag the sleds up the hill when a hand came down on her shoulder. Who . . . ? She turned—it was Ashley the snoop. "Excuse me," Ashley said. "I've been trying to work up my nerve all day, and I was just wondering . . . Can I ask you a favor?"

"What?" Kate was wary. Ashley had started the whole thing with the twenty-dollar bill and how Kate was rich as a bank. She was not only snoopy, she was a champion blabber.

"My mom's bowling group is having a fund-raiser auction? For cancer? And Mom said I had to ask you if you could get us an autographed picture. Like, from your uncle?"

Kate thought the bowling group must be pretty desperate if they wanted an autographed picture of a guy on used-car commercials. "Well, I guess so. But are you sure? I mean it's not like he's that good-looking or anything."

"You don't think he's good-looking?" Another girl, Megan, had overheard.

"You're kidding." Madison was listening, too.

"Well, maybe if he's just your old uncle, it's different," Tiffany piped up.

Kate was getting a funny feeling. "But none of you has ever *seen* my uncle."

They all started talking at once, contradicting her. Even Minh Duc. "Oh, yes," she said. "I have seen *Top Gun* and *Mission: Impossible* and that new one—"

"But no, wait! My uncle's just—*Oh!*" In a flash, Kate understood. She had never thought about how her uncle's name, *Tom Kooze*, sounded so much like *Tom Cruise*. It was spelled different, and *he* was so different. But that must be why they were mixed up. *"You guys!"* She was practically shouting, which did not help her quiet image any. When they were finally listening, she explained.

Even then, Madison argued, "But *you* told us—"

"I did not! You heard me wrong!"

"Form a line for the sleds, please," Mr. Clouse said, and the girls drifted away, all except Minh Duc. Kate could hear whispered conversations as they spread the news:

"Her uncle isn't Tom Cruise at all."

"He isn't?"

"She just made that up."

"I knew it. She thinks she's so cool."

"And she's a liar, too."

"I knew it."

"Don't feel bad." It was a second before she realized that that was Minh Duc, talking to her. "It isn't your fault. They are disappointed. It was neat, you know? Like we knew a movie star, too."

When Kate smiled, she felt the icicle scar, like a dent in her eyebrow.

"Next!" Preston, one of Ryan's buddies, held out a sled.

"Go ahead," Kate told Minh Duc.

"No, *you*." This made them both laugh.

"Well, if no one else wants it, I will take it," Mr. Clouse said.

Preston almost dropped the sled. "You sure you wanna do this, Mr. C?"

"Just give me some room." He settled into the sled and waited for Preston to push him, but Preston just scratched his head. "I dunno if this is a good idea."

"Well, I do!" Ryan came forward and heaved Mr. Clouse's sled forward with a jerk. Down he zoomed, a little unsteady with the sudden start, but by the time he hit the bump in the middle, he had righted himself, and he let out a whoop as loud as any the kids produced. When he came to rest in the snowbank at the bottom, he raised his fists, and the whole class cheered.

Minh Duc shook her head. "And he must be a hundred years old!"

"Amazing," Kate agreed. She was thinking, shoot, if *old* people can do this, I oughta be able to. Besides, even though she could see her breath, neither her nose nor her toes were asleep.

Kate took the next sled. "I'll give y'a real good push," Preston said.

"No, don't—" Kate was still untangling the rope from her boots, but he either didn't hear or chose to ignore her and off she went. Around and around the sled spun before she finally got a good grip. Then, trying to straighten out, she tipped, her legs went up in the air, and she almost somersaulted. She spun her feet forward and got her bottom in place just in time to hit the bump, fly up and land with a thud. *Bounce*—at least she was going forward. The speed took her breath away. The cold air made her eyes water, stung her cheeks and whistled in her ears. At last she hit the snowbank and jerked gracelessly to a stop.

She was shaky jogging up with the sled. At the top, she handed it to Minh Duc, who hesitated and took a deep breath before she sat down.

"Pretty wild ride," Preston said, as they watched Minh slide away. "How'dja like it?"

"I *loved* it!" Kate was amazed to hear the words come out of her mouth. "And next time, let me give *you* a real good push."

Kate was exhausted that night, from sledding and from all the turmoil after. Still, she wanted to talk to Molly one more time before she told her parents she was going home.

Gramma was on a cruise to the Galápagos Islands, so

Kate was surprised when she picked up the phone and heard Mom's voice: "I'll be off in a minute."

"Hi, Katie. How're you?" It was Uncle Tom-who-wasn't-Tom-Cruise.

How she was was more than she had the energy to explain, so Kate just said, "Fine." Then Uncle Tom told her that Mom had called to trade diet tips.

"*Tom!*"

"Oh, Angie, don't be so sensitive. From what I hear, all the women back there are chubbettes anyway. You wanna fit in, don't you?"

Kate hung up quick, before Mom had a chance to answer. She didn't want to hear any more about the size ten jeans. She agreed with Daddy: Mom looked good. And anyway, Kate had her own stuff to worry about.

If I write a letter now, Molly will have it Saturday, Monday at the latest, she thought. I can always call, too.

Dear Molly,

How are you?

I'm desperate, like usual. You will think I'm crazy to ask again, but please tell me for totally sure that everything is fine with your mom and dad. I know you said so on the phone, but I think you said "mostly."

Molly, don't take this wrong, but sometimes you tell me everything's going to work out fine when every-

thing is not going to work out fine. Like remember when you said I should skate without the wrist pads because they looked dorky?

Now I am going to tell you what happened today at school. It will help you understand how bad it is here. Maybe if your dad still doesn't want to feed me, you could show it to him so he understands.

My friend Minh Duc (I told you about her, right?) was sledding at PE today, and she isn't very good at it because she's, like, a klutz. So she closed her eyes and ran into a tree, and it was so scary!!! There was blood all over her face!!! Mr. Clouse told me to go with her to the nurse, and she was crying and we got there and the nurse was cleaning her up when Mr. Payne-in-the-neck came in to see what the noise was about. (I told you about him, right?) He still has that brace on. You would think even an old guy's neck would have healed by now.

So the nurse explained what happened, and Mr. Payne-in-the-neck goes, "I'll speak to Clouse about this. We can't have these Asian children sledding."

And I guess my eyes practically popped out of my head, and even though my family's in enough trouble with Mr. Payne, I go, "What does that mean?"

"They weren't born to it," he goes. "Simple matter of climate and genetics. We can't expect them to learn winter sports."

I was afraid Minh Duc would start crying again because she's, like, shy. But instead she goes, real quiet, "That's racist, Mr. Payne."

I was too mad to be quiet. I practically hollered, "That is the dumbest thing I ever heard!"

The nurse told me to calm down, and Mr. Payne looked like smoke was going to come out of his ears. "I don't know about students in California, Miss Sommers, but students in Belletoona don't speak to their principal that way. You'd better not let me catch you—" That's when Mr. Clouse came in, and I'm scared to think what would have happened if he hadn't.

So then when Mr. Clouse took us back to class (I am not done yet!!!) everybody was buzzing because it turned out when they were coming in from sledding, Tiffany (I told you about her, right?) sneaked down to the first-grade bathroom for a quick smoke, and Mrs. Ketchum (I didn't tell you about her, but it doesn't matter) caught her. Emma said Mr. Payne was gonna give her a swat with the paddle he keeps behind his desk and send her home and she won't be able to sit down for a month, but I don't know if that's true because Emma is not that reliable. Ryan said the school makes anybody caught smoking pay a $100 fine. Sam said she was suspended, but somebody else said she was expelled, which means suspended for the rest of your life.

Anyway, I didn't say a word, but inside I was ecstatic until after school when Tiffany's friend Madison and this other girl, Ashley the snoop, came up to me and they go: "We know you snitched."

And I go: "I did not, and why do you think I did?"

And they go: "Hardly anybody knows about the first-grade bathroom, but you came down there that time before we knew what a stuck-up, lying snitch you are."

These girls are so sweet!!! (Not!!!) So as soon as I hear from you I have to tell my parents and then I have to leave quick because now the principal and these girls are all out to get me.

Your best friend always,

Kate

Chapter Thirteen

Thursday, January 15, Belletoona, Pennsylvania: Snow squalls turning to freezing rain and sleet. Windy.

"Look at the snow! Look at the snow!" Danielle cried. They were suiting up for school. Kate could not think of anything more totally boring than falling snow, but she looked outside anyway.

"It looks like the angels are having a pillow fight," Danielle said. "The snowflakes are the feathers, see?"

Mom tugged Danielle's zipper. "That's very imaginative, honey."

Kate shook her head. My little sister is as bad as my dad, she thought. She'll grow up and bore her kids to death with stories about the wonderful winters of her childhood. Only their aunt Kate will tell the truth: Winter is the worst.

"Now, remember, Kate," Mom said. "I've got that interview later, and then I'm taking Danielle to ballet. You can walk home as usual. I hope the weather's not too bad." Mom took the front-door key off her keychain and handed it to Kate so she could let herself in. "One of these days I'll remember to get myself a duplicate key."

Mom's interview was for some kind of job. She had explained yesterday, but Kate was too distracted to pay that much attention. Now she nodded and thought: If I live that long. She was pretty sure Madison would try to get back at her, even though it was so obvious she hadn't snitched. Nobody even needed to snitch. Half the time Tiffany totally reeked of cigarettes, and Mrs. Ketchum had been watching that first-grade bathroom forever.

As Dad drove them to school, Kate looked out the window at the Great Walls of Belletoona. Everybody's settling in, she thought. Danielle's starting ballet lessons after school. Mom's got her big jeans, and now she's looking for a job. They had even invited the Douglas family over for dinner Saturday.

The car swung into the school parking lot, and Kate adjusted her backpack. If I was staying, I'd have to settle in, too. Maybe Minh Duc could come over to do homework. And if Dad and Danielle were going sledding, maybe I'd go. Sledding is okay. But, of course—she pushed the car door open and kissed her dad good-bye—I'm *not* staying.

In class, Kate hung up her backpack and her coat as usual. She half noticed when Madison came in and put her stuff on the next hook. But then Minh Duc whispered something about how Mr. Payne-in-the-neck might get in trouble for what he said about Asians the day before, and Kate didn't think anything else about backpacks—until later.

At the break, Kate headed for the bathroom. Ever since Tiffany turned the lights out on her, she avoided it before school. But sometimes she still needed pep talks.

"You're worried about Madison? Fuhgetabout her! She's a moron!" said the voice of Noah. "Now get in there, and—"

But for once Noah was wrong. Kate heard the click that meant the hall door was about to open, and she hastily turned on the water. When she glanced up in the mirror, she jumped. Mr. Payne was standing in the doorway.

"What are you doing in the girls' bathroom?" she asked. It wasn't a very smart thing to say, but he looked so funny, it popped out.

"Equally appropriate for me to ask what *you're* doing here." His smug look made Kate nervous.

"Uh . . . I'm a girl." Kate tried to make her voice respectful. Mr. Payne hated her family because of his neck, hated her in particular after yesterday. There was no telling what he might do to her if he had the chance.

The principal opened his mouth but was interrupted by a flush. Jenny, who was almost as quiet as Minh Duc, came out of a stall and shrieked when she saw the principal in the doorway. "Go about your business," he said to her, but a blush had erased his smug expression.

"Yes, sir," Jenny said, then hesitated, as if wondering if she should wash or just get the heck outta there. Finally she splashed water on her hands, shook them and bolted past Mr. Payne into the hallway.

"I'd like a look in that backpack of yours," Mr. Payne said when Jenny was gone.

"Sure." That was a relief. The only things in there were lip balm, a hairbrush, a notebook and her lunch. Nothing criminal, unless her mom had tried making bread again. Kate fumbled with the buckle, then realized it was already open. That was weird. Hadn't she closed it?

"Give it here," Mr. Payne said impatiently. He took the backpack from her, pulled the flap up and reached inside. "Just as I thought." His expression half snarl, half smile, he held up an open pack of Virginia Slims.

Kate's jaw dropped. "Those aren't—" she started to argue, but one look at Mr. Payne's face and she could see it was no use.

Madison. She had gotten revenge all right: unbuckled

Kate's pack before school and dropped in the cigarettes. At the break, she must have gone to the office and told the secretary Kate was in the bathroom smoking. No surprise Mr. Payne wanted the pleasure of nailing her himself— even if he had to come into the girls' bathroom to do it.

"Go back to your room and get the rest of your things," he said. "Then meet me in my office."

"What—What are you going to—?"

"Never mind. You'll see soon enough. We don't hold with smoking here in Belletoona, Pennsylvania—as your friend Tiffany discovered yesterday."

The next minutes were the worst of Kate's life. A jumble of anxious questions assaulted her: What would her parents say? Would they believe she was smoking? Most horrible of all, what was Mr. Payne going to do? Was it true about the paddle? Was there really a hundred-dollar fine? If she had to pay it, she'd never have the money for airfare by Valentine's Day.

When Kate walked into Room 29, everybody looked up. "Young lady?" Mr. Clouse wanted to know why she was late.

"I—I have to go—" Kate gulped, and then she heard stifled giggling. Madison and Ashley could hardly control themselves. Ryan's mouth was clamped shut, but the corners puckered. He was in on it, too.

"Go where?"

"Mr. Payne's office. He—I—I'm in trouble."

It seemed to Kate there was no sympathy in the faces of her classmates. Maybe they were all in on it. After all, Tiffany was the most popular girl there. And who was Kate Sommers? The stuck-up, lying, outsider snitch.

Even Minh Duc was looking down at her desk—like she's ashamed she ever talked to me, Kate thought. Kate felt her face flush, hands turn clammy, knees weaken. She was almost dizzy with humiliation. She had tried so hard not to be noticed, and here she was being laughed at by the whole sixth grade.

Mr. Clouse's face was puzzled. "Do you want to tell me what's going on?" he asked.

Kate shook her head. What could he do anyway? Mr. Payne was his boss, right?

The teacher raised his hands as if he surrendered. "All right, then," he said. "We'll look forward to having you back."

Maybe *you* will, Kate thought. As the door closed behind her, she heard a burst of laughter, and a squeaky voice called, "Bye-*bye*, California!"

Kate never once looked up as she walked down the long hallway, just focused on the gray squares of linoleum passing under her feet. What would Mr. Payne do to her?

She stopped short when she reached the school lobby. *Great.* She was looking so hard at the floor, she had walked right by the office. Through the glass entrance doors, she saw the snow swirling in the wind outside. For once, she wished she were out in it. She felt like a prisoner about to face the warden—only she wasn't locked in. She could just walk right out those doors. . . .

Right, Kate thought. Seconds were ticking away. Time to turn around and face whatever was coming to her. But she didn't turn around, just stood there watching the snow and remembering Mr. Payne's snarl, the unfriendly faces of her classmates, and that squeaky, "Bye-*bye*, California."

Then she was pulling on her coat, pushing the heavy glass doors, feeling the wind sting her eyes and the snowflakes pat her nose, walking fast toward the school gate, wondering if this was how a bank robber felt on his way to the getaway car. Act natural. Don't run. *Are they after me yet?*

She was all the way to the corner before she said to herself: Kate Sommers, what are you doing? What have you done?

And what are you going to do now?

Chapter Fourteen

"Pittsburgh International Airport advises travelers departing Thursday, January fifteen, to expect moderate delays due to accumulations of snowfall on runways. No flight cancellations are anticipated at this time."

Kate Sommers was on the lam. Thinking back, she wasn't sure when she had decided to do this. Had she really decided at all?

The walk home from school had been almost unbearable. By the time she got to the corner, the harmless snowflakes had turned into rain so cold the drops froze the instant they hit anything. Soon every surface—from sidewalk to tree bark—was covered with ice.

Kate had been convinced someone was following her. Any second she thought she would hear a police siren or, worse, Mr. Payne's voice shouting at her to get back to his office right now. Once she looked behind her and saw a man with a beard. *Mr. Payne!* She took a running step, lost her footing on the icy sidewalk and sat down hard. The man caught up to her and offered his hand. Kate didn't dare look at his face, but she caught a glimpse of his neck. No brace. It wasn't Mr. Payne at all.

At the bottom of her hill, she had stepped off a curb into a half-frozen puddle, and a gush of water sloshed into her boots, soaking through both pairs of socks. Then a car came up fast—the police? Mr. Payne? Neither one, but the tires had sent a fountain of dirty snow and ice splashing from the roadway. Now she was drenched from head to toe.

Shivering, caked with icy grime, aching from her fall, she had trudged on toward her house. Maybe that's when it hit her: The time for Operation Defrost was now. If she ran, she would never have to face Mr. Payne or Madison or Ryan or any of them again. She wouldn't even have to face her parents. Mom was at the job interview and wouldn't be back until late—after Danielle's ballet lesson.

She had unlocked the front door with Mom's key and looked at her watch. With the time difference, it was still early enough to catch Molly before school. If there was a bus to Pittsburgh that afternoon, a flight to Los Angeles that night . . .

Her parents would forgive her, wouldn't they?

The phone was ringing. Automatically, she went to answer it, then realized it was probably school looking for her. Three rings, four rings, five rings—*click*. The answering machine picked up. Kate lifted the receiver and dropped it back before whoever it was could leave a message. Then she took it off the hook again so they couldn't call back.

When had she become such a good sneak?

From then on, everything went smoothly, like it was always meant to happen this way. Kate called the airline, and there was a seat on the flight from Pittsburgh at 6:30. She gulped when she heard the price—more than twice what she expected. But she could earn the rest when she got home to California. Wasn't she an experienced baby-sitter? For now, it was easy to read Mom's credit card number off the statement on her desk.

Then she called Molly, who was both home and allowed to talk. She sounded surprised but said sure, *chica*, she'd be at the airport for her best friend. No problemation. She'd tell her mom to get the bed ready. No need to mention that Kate hadn't exactly cleared it with her parents yet. And don't worry, everything will work out fine.

Kate had taken a shower and packed her duffel bag; she had to dig deep in her drawers for T-shirts, shorts, and a bathing suit. When she looked at her watch again, it was noon already. Not much time till the bus left. Quickly, she had written a note:

Dear Mom and Dad,
   Please don't worry about me. I am okay. And please don't believe anything you hear about me from Mr. Payne or anybody else at school. It is all a lie.
   I will call you tomorrow. I am sorry to leave like this but I have to. I will explain everything as soon as I can.
   I will see you as soon as I graduate from high school, or maybe you can visit before that. I love you. It isn't your fault.
   Love always,

   Kate

Now where to leave it? Not on the kitchen table or any obvious place. Mom might find it too soon and try to stop her. Kate finally decided to put it on her own pillow, with the front-door key. Sooner or later, Mom would come into Kate's room looking for her. She set the note down, read it over, realized something was missing and wrote:

P.S. — Tell Dani I even love her.

*   *   *

The heater on the bus was broken.

Kate didn't have her mittens. When the taxi came she ran out of the house so fast she forgot them, but anyway she would never need mittens once she got to Isla Nada. So now, an hour out of Belletoona, she crossed her arms over her chest and wiggled her fingers in her armpits. Her hideous red coat was still damp from the drenching on the walk home, and she could feel her fingers freezing stiff. Her toes, scrunched in boots and two pairs of wool socks, had already turned to ice cubes.

"Sorry about the temperature, ladies and gentlemen," the driver's voice crackled over the speaker. "But I am pleased to announce that no snowfall is currently expected inside the bus."

Very funny, Kate thought. And what was "ladies and gentlemen" supposed to mean? She looked over her shoulder. Besides herself, there were exactly two women on the bus and no gentlemen at all.

She wished Noah would give her a pep talk, but Noah seemed to have abandoned her. Kate realized suddenly that no one she knew had any idea where she was at this moment. She was out here in the middle of the Pennsylvania nowhere, completely alone.

"I'm doing the right thing," Kate whispered to herself. "I can't live in this place. I have to go *home*."

She closed her eyes and tried to imagine the brightness of Isla Nada: blue water, blue sky, green palm trees, green lawns, pink flowers. Unfortunately, no sooner had the beach come into focus than the channel changed and there was her mom. In Kate's imagination, it was several hours from now. Mom had just gotten home and was looking at her watch, her forehead wrinkled up with worry. She hadn't found the note yet—where could Kate be? It wasn't like she had friends or anything. Mom tried calling the Douglas's house.

"Kate? No, Kate didn't come over after school. Just a minute, let me ask Peter," Mrs. Douglas would say. Then, "He said 'unh unh,' which I take to mean he hasn't seen her. I'm sorry. Let me know if I can help."

Kate tried to change the channel, but Mom seemed to be on all of them. *Click*—there was Mom finding the note on her pillow. *Click*—Mom crying on Dad's shoulder.

To shut the inner TV off, Kate opened her eyes and looked beyond the driver to the sleet dappling the windshield. What if the storm got worse and they didn't get to the airport on time? Or what if the plane couldn't take off?

I'll walk if I have to, Kate thought. This time tomorrow, I'll be soaking up sunshine on the beach, listening to the surf, wearing a bathing suit instead of eleven layers of underwear. She thought about the delicious combination of hot sand and cool, splashing water, but it didn't make her feel better. It made her shiver.

          *   *   *

"But—where are we?" The ride was so dull that, cold as she was, Kate must have dozed. The squeak of brakes startled her. When the other two passengers brushed by on their way to the door, she realized the bus had stopped for good.

Now Kate was standing outside in the blowing snow while the driver reached into the luggage space under the bus for her duffel bag.

"We're in Pittsburgh, Miss. That's where you wanted to go, isn't it?"

"But . . . where's the airport?"

"Airport! About twenty miles from here. We're smack downtown now. You wanted the *airport*?"

Kate nodded miserably. Everything had gone perfectly—until now. How could she have been so stupid? But here she was, stuck at some old building in a strange city.

"Do your parents know where you are?" the driver asked. Kate read the name tag on his pocket: Mr. Sam Rudolph. He held on to her bag.

"Sure. Of course they do." She felt the blood rushing to her face as she lied. Would he notice? Mr. Sam Rudolph cocked his head skeptically, so she kept talking, "I—I'm going to see my gramma. In California."

"And your parents—they didn't know the airport was west of town?"

"I guess not."

"Hmm," he said, "don't sound kosher to me, but I guess your business is your business." He handed her the bag. She locked her frozen fingers around the handle and looked through the windows into the building. Two sleepy-looking people bundled in coats sat in orange plastic chairs. Beyond them was a dark snack bar. It didn't look any warmer inside than out.

How was she going to get to the airport? Kate didn't think the money left in her wallet was enough for a twenty-mile taxi ride, and anyway, she didn't see any taxis. Josh used to hitchhike sometimes, but that was too dangerous.

She looked at her watch — 5:05. The flight was at 6:30.

"Tell ya what," the driver said. "There's a big hotel, not far. Has an airport bus. Costs somethin', I'm not sure what. I could give you a lift on my way home."

Kate was so grateful she almost blurted yes. But then she realized that that would be accepting a ride from a stranger. A strange *man*. He looked fine. Kind even. But creepy people looked okay sometimes. They told you that in school.

"I—I can't," she said. "I mean, that's really nice and everything, but it would be—I mean, my mom says I shouldn't—"

"Suit yourself, Miss." Mr. Sam Rudolph shrugged.

"Seems to me your mom got you into this pickle, though. She ought to've found out where the airport was before she put you on the bus."

He turned away. Kate watched his retreating back for a few seconds and made a snap decision. It might be risky, but she didn't have any choice. "Mister!"

He turned around and clapped his gloved hands, scattering snowflakes.

"I'll go! I'll go with you."

"Well, come on then. My wife waits dinner for me. The kids'll be half starved by the time I get there."

Kate followed him, dragging her heavy duffel bag on the ground. She felt a little better that he had mentioned kids. Creeps didn't have kids, did they?

Mr. Sam Rudolph brushed snow off the windshield, then opened the passenger door for her. It was a small car, clean on the inside like he vacuumed it a lot. That was a good sign, too, wasn't it? Unless it meant he was lying about the kids. People with kids never had clean cars, did they? She buckled her seat belt and asked, "How far is it—to the hotel, I mean?"

He started the engine. "Not far. Tell ya the truth, I don't usually get much beyond the bus station when I'm downtown. We live on the North Side. I may have to zig and zag a little to find the front entrance. What time's your flight?"

Kate's heart felt like a lump in her chest. What did that

mean, zig and zag? Was he telling her that so she wouldn't get suspicious when he took her someplace else? The car pulled into traffic, and Kate looked at the door handle. If they came to a red light, she could jump out.

"Cat got your tongue?" Mr. Sam Rudolph glanced over at her. "I said, what time's your flight?"

"Uh . . . I'll make it." She didn't know why, but she didn't want to tell him any more than she had to. She glanced over at his face, flashing light and dark in the oncoming headlights. They were so close together in the little car, she could see the bristles of beard on his chin. She could even smell him, some kind of mediciney smell. Soap maybe. She didn't think she had ever been this close to a stranger before.

The car pulled onto an on-ramp and then some kind of freeway. No stoplights. Kate looked out the window. The river below was shiny black. Kate could hear blood pulsing in her ears.

Please let me see the hotel soon, she thought.

Please let Mr. Sam Rudolph not be a creep.

"Why, honey, you're white as a sheet!" He must have been watching her. The car had warmed up, and Kate felt hot in her jacket. What if he reached over and touched her? Or locked the door?

"I'm okay." Kate choked on the words. Why had she accepted a ride? Now she was trapped.

Suddenly Mr. Sam Rudolph laughed. It was loud in

the small car, and Kate jumped. He wasn't just a creep, he was a *maniac*! From TV, Kate knew about maniacs and young girls. She wanted to scream, but she couldn't gulp enough air to get the sound out.

"You're scared!" Mr. Sam Rudolph said through his laughter. "Of *me*! Oh, Miss, I'm sorry." He wiped his eyes. "You took a ride from somebody you don't know, and now you've scared yourself half to death! Honey, everything's okay. I don't got a knife in the glove compartment or nothin'. Go ahead and check if you want. And look here—here's the hotel. I didn't even have to zigzag."

It was true. Kate could see the name outlined in white lights. The car headed down the off-ramp toward the big glass-and-concrete building. A few seconds later, Mr. Sam Rudolph pulled up to the curb, and the car was filled with light that spilled from the entrance. A man in a fancy uniform opened her door.

Kate was so relieved that the tension drained away, and left her bones like jelly. "Thank you," she breathed.

"Don't mention it," said Mr. Sam Rudolph.

Somehow she mustered the strength to push the door open and yank her duffel bag from the backseat. Mr. Sam Rudolph waved her off, still chuckling. "Oh, is my wife gonna *laugh*."

Inside, the lobby was bright, bustling, and warm. It was

weird, but just surviving the agony with Mr. Sam Rudolph made Kate feel better. Like she could handle anything. She marched over to a desk marked Concierge and asked about a bus to the airport.

"Where are your parents, honey?" the woman asked.

"Upstairs." Lying was getting easier. "They told me to come down and find out."

"Kind of a heavy bag for you, isn't it?"

Kate felt like screaming, but she took a breath instead. "I can manage."

"Give it to the bellman there." The woman nodded toward a man with a luggage cart. "He'll put it on the van for you. Next one leaves at five-thirty, ten minutes." The woman looked back at the papers on the desk.

"Uh . . . how much does it cost?" Kate asked.

The woman looked up. Was she suspicious again? "Didn't your dad put it on the room bill?"

"No, he didn't." Now Kate was mad. Just let me get out of here! she thought.

"Pay the driver then." The woman looked back at her papers. Maybe she didn't believe Kate, but she didn't quiz her anymore. "Twenty dollars."

Kate had enough money, then. She would even have a few dollars extra to buy something for Josh at the airport. Dragging her duffel bag, she walked over to the bellman. "Airporter?" he asked.

Kate nodded but didn't say anything. Everybody she talked to seemed like a spy from the world of grown-ups, a spy who wanted to imprison her forever in Pennsylvania.

After she paid the driver, she didn't say a word to anybody on the van, didn't even smile when a passenger who looked like Gramma smiled at her. When they rolled off the freeway and past a big Pittsburgh International Airport sign, the driver looked back at Kate and asked, "Domestic or international?"

"What?" She didn't know what he meant.

"Tell him where you're going, dear," the Gramma lady said gently.

"Los Angeles," Kate snapped. Her voice was so rude she hardly recognized it.

"Well, thank *you*," the driver said sarcastically.

The lady's sweet expression soured. Kate was so ashamed she wished she could disappear. She wanted to tell the lady her real gramma loved her a lot and she was really a very nice girl. No matter what Mr. Payne thought. No matter what Tiffany and Madison and the entire sixth-grade class at Byrd Elementary School thought. But of course she couldn't. Anyway, now the lady probably wouldn't believe her.

When I'm home, everything will be all right, Kate thought. I just have to get *home*.

As she pushed the revolving door into the terminal,

Kate heard the loudspeaker: "Final boarding call for US Airways flight one-two-three for Los Angeles. All passengers should be . . ."

Should be what? Kate's watch said 6:10. She should have twenty minutes, right? She scooped up her bag in both arms and stumbled to the counter under the US Airways sign.

"I've got—" She was breathless. "I've got a reservation for Los Angeles."

The agent punched something into her computer and shook her head. "One-two-three? That flight's closed, Miss."

"Oh *please*," Kate said. "I've just got to—"

"Okay, okay. Let me call down there and see."

The agent turned away and Kate could hear only mumbling, but when she hung up she gave Kate a smile and a thumbs-up. "Stay right here while I print out the ticket and order a cart. You'll have to carry the bag."

Moments later, people were scattering out of the way as Kate zoomed through the airport on a motorized cart that flashed a yellow light and beeped. She was going to make it. She was. And Molly would be at the airport in L.A., and everything was going to be okay. No problemation, *chica*.

The man at Gate 16 was waving when the cart pulled up.

Kate handed him the ticket, grinning because she was

in time. "We held it for you," he said sternly. "Isn't anybody seeing you off?"

Suddenly she was worried again. "I'm old enough."

"Go on, go on." He handed the ticket back. "I'll bring the bag."

Kate jogged down the jetway, with the gate agent on her heels. "Take any empty seat," the flight attendant said. As soon as the bag was handed over, the attendant pulled down the hatch and latched it.

The plane was nearly full, and everybody looked up and watched as Kate walked down the aisle. Nobody smiled. When Kate finally saw an empty seat, she had to practically crawl over a man in a business suit to get to it.

"Excuse me, I'm sorry," she mumbled. The man was reading a magazine and didn't say anything, just moved his knees to let her by.

Kate dropped into the seat and closed her eyes. *I made it,* she said to herself. Mr. Payne can't stop me. Mom can't stop me. Nothing can stop me. I'm going home.

"Good evening, ladies and gentlemen," said the loudspeaker. "We've just had word from the tower that a bit of snowfall's accumulated on the runway. We'll be experiencing a short delay while the equipment gets that cleared. In the meantime, relax, sit back, and thank you for flying US Airways."

Some of the passengers groaned. Kate blinked her eyes open and looked at her watch. After all this, would it be the miserable Pennsylvania winter that stopped her? Mom and Danielle should be home soon. What would happen when they found the note? What if they called the bus company or, worse, the airline? What if they called the police?

One of the flight attendants was walking down the aisle toward her. If her parents had called, would she get yanked off the plane? After all she'd been through, the humiliation would kill her. The flight attendant stopped and leaned over the man in the business suit. *Oh no*, Kate thought. *This is it. Yanked.* Her heart was pounding.

"I put your bag in the closet up front. You can get it as you're deplaning."

Kate breathed again. "Thank you. Thank you *very* much."

The speaker hissed and clicked. "Uh . . . ladies and gentlemen, this is First Officer Frost again. The tower tells us the runway's clear, and they've got three planes ahead of us for takeoff. We'll be pulling away from the gate here shortly. You'll be happy to hear the weather's clear over the rest of the country this evening. These snowy conditions seem to be isolated in western Pennsylvania."

A moment later, the plane lurched and began rolling backward. As long as we're on the ground, they could still stop us, Kate thought. I won't be happy until we're in the air. But when the plane lifted off, she still couldn't relax.

She had seen the flight attendants talking on a phone near the cockpit. Could the police call on that? Would they put her in handcuffs? Turn the plane around? Make it land someplace she never heard of?

There was a movie, but Kate was too worried to follow the plot. Every time she felt a bump, she expected an unscheduled landing. And every time a flight attendant came near, she closed her eyes so that she wouldn't see the handcuffs.

She thought about the last time she was on an airplane, when she and Dani and Mom had flown to Pennsylvania. She had fought the whole time with her sister and driven Mom crazy, but she remembered a weird sort of peace, too. She had vowed to make the best of things — until Operation Defrost, of course. And she had made the best of things, hadn't she?

Hadn't she?

After the movie, they served crackers and fruit, but Kate couldn't eat. Then she tried to sleep, but when she closed her eyes she saw reruns of Channel Mom. By the time the plane landed in Los Angeles, Kate was so tired she could hardly see. Dragging her duffel bag, which had never seemed so heavy, she walked down the jetway toward home.

Chapter Fifteen

Friday, January 15, Isla Nada, California: Overnight lows in the 50s, Friday, night and early morning low clouds burning off by midday. Highs in the mid to upper 70s.

"**K**ate! Over here! Golly, you're so pale!"

Kate heard Molly's voice clearly, but the crowd of faces in the airport was just a blur. It was only 8:30 P.M. L.A. time, 11:30 in Belletoona. She felt like she'd been up all night.

"Where . . . ?" Kate looked around.

"Over here, *chica*!" Molly came into focus, waving both arms over her head. Really, it was a wonder Kate hadn't spotted her right away. She was wearing a sleeveless magenta jumpsuit and turquoise sandals. Seeing her,

Kate felt overstuffed, hot and sticky. She wished she could peel off her coat, her sweater, her turtleneck, even her wool socks.

"Here, Josh, get her bag, for golly sakes! Wait'll you *hear* about all the trouble we had getting to the airport! My mom'll kill me, but that's okay because, as of today after school, I'm grounded for like two months, so what else . . ." Molly never stopped talking as she hugged Kate and pulled the bag away from her to hand over to Josh.

Josh!

Molly kept talking, but Kate couldn't take her eyes off him. For the moment, everything else was forgotten. He was even more gorgeous in the flesh than he had been in her memory—incredible tan, pale hair, big eyes. She had been dreaming of him so long that seeing him made her feel shy. Molly was so nice to bring him with her! "I didn't know *you* were coming," she said quietly.

"Yeah, well," he said, like he felt shy, too. "Here I am."

She stepped toward him for a kiss—at least a hug—but he just smiled that dreamy smile and jerked his head toward the exit. "Let's go. I'll carry this. Man, it's like heavy as a board."

". . . so you remember Mandy, right? It was all her fault really, but *try* to convince my mother! Like, you'd think it was *armed robbery* instead of a crummy pair of purple underwear! So the next day . . ."

As they walked, Kate tried to follow Molly's story. It had something to do with shoplifting, or maybe trading clothes. Anyway, she got the idea that Molly's mom had had a cow over something and didn't drive them to the airport. They had had to get the Pink Shuttle, same as Molly's dad did when he went away on business.

Beep-beep—one of the little airport carts whooshed by.

"I went on one of those," Kate said.

Molly was still talking and didn't hear. "Oh yeah?" said Josh. "Cool."

"Well, it wasn't really because I was really late for the plane. I, like, almost didn't make it."

"Sheesh. That woulda been bad," Josh said. "I mean, it was a bunch o' trouble to get here. I'm gonna be, like, *tired* in the water tomorrow morning."

"You still surf every morning?"

He looked at her sideways, like he couldn't believe she would ask such a question. "Well, *yeah*."

"I'm sorry," Kate said. "It's just . . . I feel like I've been gone forever, like everything should've changed. Does that make sense?"

"I guess," said Josh. "Don't you want to take your coat off or something? It looks like somebody's old sleeping bag."

"Nice guy." Kate tried to make it sound like a joke. "Aren't I cute anymore?" She wouldn't mind a hint that maybe he still cared.

He smiled again, but that was all. What is with him, anyway? Kate wondered. He didn't have to come to the airport. Who asked him? She kept her coat on. She expected it to be cool outside, but when they stepped out of the terminal, the air was balmy.

Molly disagreed. "Brrrrrr. Can you believe this frozenation?" she said. "Look" — she held out her arm — "goosebumps! This must be what it's like in Bell-fishcake, huh?"

"Belle*toona*," Kate said automatically. Suddenly everything about them was bugging her. Weren't they even glad to see her? They didn't act like it.

Without Noah, she had to talk to herself. Settle down, Kate, she said. Molly is your best friend. She came all the way to the airport to meet you — *and* she brought Josh, even if he is acting weird, which isn't Molly's fault.

"Oh, look! It's there, come on!" Molly pointed across the street. The Pink Shuttle van was sitting at the curb. She and Josh ran ahead to catch it. Kate, weighed down by her coat, was a few steps behind. By the time she got to them, the doors were folding shut and she had to push through. Beneath her long underwear, a dribble of sweat ran down her side. *Gross.*

Inside the van, Molly and Josh took seats next to each other, leaving Kate a place a row back beside another passenger, a man with a beard who seemed to be asleep. Kate did a double-take — *It couldn't be . . . ?* It wasn't. This man didn't have a neck brace either. She was going crazy.

Only in movies did the bad guy follow the hero almost three thousand miles—*and* get there first.

Kate sat down, thinking it was kind of rude for Molly and Josh to sit together. I mean, *I'm* the one who's been away forever. But when the van pulled out, Molly swiveled her head around and grinned. "It's great to see you!" she said. "You're pale as a *ghost*, but a few days on the beach will take care of that, right?"

"Right!" Kate grinned back. She felt better. They were still best friends.

The van stopped a couple more times, but there were no more passengers. Then it headed down Airport Boulevard and onto the 405 freeway toward Isla Nada. Molly must have been sleepy because she didn't say anything. Neither did Josh, but that was no surprise.

"It is so *weird* to be here. Everything looks enormo!" Kate said to the backs of Molly's and Josh's heads. "Bellotoona is dinky," she went on. "Everybody knows everybody. Did I tell you the doctor who stitched up my face is the mom of this girl, Madison . . ." Kate told about how Madison set her up and she got caught with the cigarettes, and how she half expected to see Mr. Payne-in-the-neck on some corner in Isla Nada. As she talked, she noticed that Molly's head was bobbing. Finally, it fell to rest on Josh's shoulder.

"Hey—Hey, wake up!" Kate's voice was so shrill she startled the man next to her. "Pipe down," he grumped.

"Sorry." Kate waited a minute, then jiggled Josh's shoulder. "Molly," she whispered.

"It's okay," Josh said. "Let her alone."

Kate knew she was being ridiculous, but she really didn't like seeing her best friend's head on her boyfriend's shoulder. She tried again. *"Molly—"*

"She's asleep, okay? Let her alone."

Kate scowled at Molly's head, willing it to flop the other way, but it stuck to Josh as if it were Velcro'd. Tired as Kate was, the beginning of a thought formed in her mind, like a bubble. She popped it. It was something bad, and her day had been hard enough.

A few minutes later, the Pink Shuttle pulled off the freeway and stopped at an apartment building. "Yo! Long Beach! You're home!" the driver hollered. The sleepy guy next to Kate looked around like he didn't know where he was, then muttered something and got up.

"Next stop—Isla Nada!" the driver said. He was so loud that he woke Molly. She looked back at Kate and tried to smile, but it came out a yawn instead.

"Not far now," Kate said in a very cheerful voice. She wanted to keep her friend awake so her head would stay where it belonged—off Josh. "I bet your mom won't be that mad. She'll be glad to see me, right? She always liked me."

"Well," Molly said, "anyway, she's gonna be surprised."

That was a funny thing to say. "You mean, like, *how* surprised?" Kate asked.

"Well . . . *surprised* surprised. You know, like—surprised you're here."

Kate refused to believe what she was hearing. *"You told me she said I could stay with you."*

"Uh . . . well . . ." Molly looked at Josh instead of Kate. "She did say that, sort of. But I think she thought it was one of those kid things? Like she could say yes and it wouldn't matter because we'd forget all about it?" She paused as if she was hoping Kate would say, No problem-ation, but Kate didn't.

"Well, anyway," she went on, "today, after you called, I was going to tell her, but there was that whole thing with the purple underwear, so I didn't, and anyway, I was grounded and I had to sneak out my window to come to the airport." She finished in a rush, "But it'll all work out okay. She'll be asleep by the time we get home, and Daddy's in Phoenix or Seattle or somewhere, and in the morning we'll think of something."

Kate fell back against the seat. "Shoot, Molly! I don't believe you! I mean, it's not like I'm coming over for *snacks*—"

"Hey, let her alone, okay?" Josh was on continuous loop.

Kate took a deep breath and squeezed her eyes shut.

No way was she gonna cry. No way. Half a second later, the tears were rolling.

"Oh, golly, I'm sorry." Molly crawled over the seat to sit next to her. "I'm really sorry. But it's not that big of a problem. If I throw a tantrum, they'll let you stay. My mom does like you. She says you're a good influence—isn't that a stitch?"

Kate choked back her sobs. She didn't want to be a total baby, especially in front—or even in back—of Josh.

"Golly, you're not gonna, like, hyperventilate or anything, are you?" Molly sounded worried. "Joshie, honey, didn't you do CPR last year?"

Joshie, honey?

The bubble Kate had tried to pop turned into a blimp: Josh is Molly's boyfriend now. Kate is history.

If Kate had been close to hysterics before, that put her over the edge.

"No!" Kate yelled, pounding her fist against the seat. "No!" And the tears gushed.

"What's goin' on back there?" The driver was watching in the mirror. "Ever'body all right?" He shook his head and muttered. "Well, o' course not. Why's it *always* on *my* run?"

"I think you better pull over." Molly had to yell to be heard over Kate.

The driver nodded and clicked the blinker on. "*Naturally*," he said. "Last run o' the night."

A few moments later, the van was parked on the shoulder of the freeway, and Kate, tears exhausted, was gasping to catch her breath. The driver knelt next to her and shook his head sympathetically. Molly blotted Kate's wet face with an old McDonald's napkin. Josh sat in his seat, looking straight ahead like the whole thing embarrassed him.

"She ran away from home," Molly explained to the driver. "She's sort of upset."

"Oh yeah, I done that. And look here." The driver tapped his chest. "I turned out okay. It was a rough ten years, but I turned out fine."

Kate barely heard him. All through this terrible trip, all through the terrible months in Belletoona, she had counted on getting home. Well, she was nearly there, but home had changed.

"I—" Kate struggled to get the words out. "I shouldn't have come back."

"Sure you shoulda." Molly kept blotting, even though Kate's face was dry. "Think about the beach. Think about skating on the walk. Think about hunting shells and the new suit you're gonna buy. It's gonna be great. Just like always."

"Can we *go*?" Josh whined.

"Honey, hush up, okay? Give her a sec."

"Yeah, hush up," the driver chimed in. "Can't you see she's upset?"

Kate took a breath and looked Molly in the eye. Her voice was steady. "You and Josh are, like . . . ?"

Molly dropped her napkin hand and her face turned red. "It's that obvious, huh? Oh, Kate—I'm sorry . . . shoot, I said that already. I mean, we were gonna tell you right away, but . . . I guess I kinda screwed up, huh? But look, it'll be okay now. It'll all be okay."

Kate took a deep breath and blinked. Then she looked at the driver. "I think we can go."

"You sure?"

Kate nodded.

It was a quiet half hour to Isla Nada. Kate's emotions were spent, and she felt nothing as they approached—not when they went by the mall, not when she saw the ocean, not even when they went by her old house, where all the windows were dark.

"You can just let us out here," Molly called when they got to a corner a block from her house.

"Climbin' in the window, huh?" The driver chuckled. "Yeah, I done that."

Out of the van, Josh handed the big duffel bag to Kate, then looked down at his huaraches and said, "I'm, like, sorry, Booboo."

"Yeah," she said.

Molly opened her mouth to say something, but he was already walking away. "See you tomorrow!" she said. Then she whispered to Kate, "Do you think he's mad?"

Kate tried to put the bag on her shoulder, but it pulled her off balance. "Who cares?" she answered. "He's a jerk."

"Yeah, you might be right. Here." Molly grabbed a strap, and they started slowly down the sidewalk under the streetlamps.

Kate looked at her watch. It was 10:30 L.A. time, 1:30 in Belletoona. She wondered if her parents were still up, if they had called the police, if they were upset . . .

They were two doors from Molly's house when Molly stopped short, yanking the bag and Kate back with her. "Oh *no!* Oh *shoot!*" she hissed. "I am, like, *dead meat.*" Kate looked up. A light was on in Molly's living room. "Mom always goes to bed early," Molly moaned, "unless she's waiting up for *me.*"

"Let's just get it over with." Kate pulled forward on the duffel bag.

Molly hung back. "Since when are you Miss Brave?"

"Since I realized things can't get any worse."

"Oh, all right." Molly started moving again. "No point going through the window now. But maybe she's asleep on the sofa. Then we can sneak by."

The door was unlocked. Mrs. Blossom, wearing a shiny black bathrobe, was sitting on the sofa, arms folded across her chest, very much awake.

"Uh . . . hi, Mom. Look who's here." Molly tried the perfect innocent approach. Her smile was as big as an alligator's.

Mrs. Blossom ignored her daughter. "I wish I could say it's nice to see you again, Kate."

"I guess it's kind of a surprise. Molly was supposed—"

"Not exactly a surprise," Mrs. Blossom interrupted. "Your mother called. I don't need to tell you she—"

"My *mother*?"

"Sometimes parents aren't quite as dumb as daughters think. She and I put two and two together when I saw Molly wasn't in her bed. At any rate, *you* will go in the kitchen and call her this instant. And *you*"—she turned to Molly and her voice got very, very quiet—"*you* will march up to your room and stay there until you turn twenty-one."

Neither girl opened her mouth; they just followed orders.

As Kate pulled the receiver off the wall, a small part of her brain, the part that still worked, told her it was good that she was totally numb. Otherwise, she would never have worked up the nerve to dial.

"Oh, thank heavens! Coldwell—*Coldwell*, pick up the phone. She's all right." Mom's voice was hoarse, like she'd been crying.

Dad came on the line, his voice raspy, too. "Katie? That you? You in California? Your mother was so worried! What *ever* possessed you—"

"—your father was *beside himself*—"

"—your poor mother . . . all these hours, crying and—"

"—the airline told us you were on the flight, but I still—"

"—and poor little Danielle . . ."

If the circumstances had been different, Kate might have smiled. Her parents were being so perfectly her parents. Anyway, it made the phone call easier. She didn't have to say anything.

"Mother! Mother! Tell her about the—" That was Dani.

"Danielle, get off the line; she's all right. We'll—"

"Tell her about the cat, Mother! Father—*tell* her! Then she'll *want* to come home!"

"What cat?" Kate asked.

"Oh, it's nothing, pip-squeak," said her dad. "Going to the pound in the morning. Now, we've called the airline, and—"

"*The pound? She is not!*" Dani sounded way more worried about this cat than she was about her own sister, which, Kate thought, made perfect sense.

"Oh, Coldwell, of course she isn't going to the pound," Mom intervened. "Kate, honey, Danielle found a cat under the basement steps this afternoon—you had the front-door key, remember? Such a sweet cat—half starved and half frozen, but we put her in your room, and she'll be fine—"

"Fine for the pound," Dad interrupted.

"Don't talk nonsense, dear." Mom paused, and there

was a moment's silence on the line. "Katie? Where'd you go?" She sounded anxious again.

"Is she a white cat?" Kate asked.

"Well, yes, as a matter of fact. How did you know?"

Danielle caught on immediately. "The phantom snowball, Mother! Why didn't I think of that? Oh, Katie, I'm sorry! It wasn't a hallucimation! You're not nutso after all! Mother"—Danielle's voice changed to a whisper—"don't tell her about her shells!"

"What about my shells?"

"You weren't supposed to hear!" Danielle protested.

"Well, honey." Mom sighed. "We put the cat in your room? And . . . I guess she was upset, and she got up on your bureau . . . knocked your collection to the floor."

"*Smithereens*," said Danielle. "But, Katie—you'll still come home, won't you?"

To Kate's amazement, the tears started again. She wouldn't have thought there were that many in her whole skull. She sniffed them back so she could talk. "Yes, Dani," she said, "I'll still come home."

Chapter Sixteen

Friday, February 13, Belletoona, Pennsylvania: Clear and warmer today. Highs in the mid 20s. Chance of snow tonight.

$\mathbf{B}$yrd Elementary School held its Valentine parties at the end of the day. At lunch there was a buzz of anticipation. Would Ryan give a Valentine to Tiffany, or was it true they broke up? Did Madison get some big lovey-dovey lacy thing for Preston, even though everybody knew Preston thought Madison was fat? Most important, did Emma's mom buy the whole class chocolate hearts again?

Kate was eating with Jenny and Minh Duc and Megan, same as she had practically every day since she had come back from California. At least they would give her valentines. Minh Duc had gone sledding with her and

Danielle last weekend—she kept her eyes open and never hit a tree. And Kate and Megan were partners for the science fair next month. Jenny, Minh Duc, and Megan were the quietest girls in the school, the quietest girls Kate had ever met. She always felt like Number One Loudmouth when she was with them.

Kate swallowed her last bite of jalapeño scone and remembered how she had been scared to move to Pennsylvania because no one would know who she was. Well, no one did. For a while she was a quiet, smart kid. Then she was a lying, stuck-up snitch. Now was she the Number One Loudmouth? She didn't know yet. Maybe you had to test yourself a few times before you found out who you were.

Of course, Molly would have had no trouble pinning a label on Kate. Molly would simply have called her a nun.

Kate had flown out of Los Angeles Sunday morning. Mrs. Blossom had let Molly out of her room long enough for the drive to the airport. Do I hate her? Kate had asked herself as they sat, stuck in traffic, on the 405. I *should* hate her.

"Nah, you shouldn't. What's to hate?" Hey—it was Noah. Welcome back, Noah. "So, she steals your boyfriend. A boyfriend who sends ya socks for Christmas? A boyfriend who treats ya like a pit stop? Not worth the aggravation, y'ask me. Just another pretty face, that guy. Now get in there—"

All right, all right. I *don't* hate her. Mostly, Molly was just too much of an optimist—like Daddy. And even when she tried to do the right thing, she got distracted before she was done doing it. As for Josh, well—Kate still got weak when she thought of how gorgeous he was. Too bad all the gorgeous was on the outside.

"I am, like, *so* sorry, *chica,*" Molly said when they got to the airport. "But hey—here. I got this for you. It's not much after all that's happened. . . . " From her purse she pulled what looked like a wad of tissue paper.

Kate unwrapped it and grinned, tears in her eyes. "The giant *Forreiria.* Now at least I'll have one shell to start my collection over. I can't believe you found one."

"Well, actually, *chica,* I bought it. But it's still a good peace offering, isn't it? I mean, I am so sorry—about Josh? And telling my parents? And even that purple underwear, but it was on sale *anyway* . . ."

"You know what?" Kate fingered the pink shell. "It's totally weird, but I think it worked out okay—just like you said. I don't think I'm supposed to live here anymore. Maybe I'm supposed to stay in Belletoona."

Molly's eyes got big. "You mean, like—and become a *nun? Forever?*"

Kate smiled. "Maybe. Right now, it doesn't sound that—"

"Ladies and gentlemen," the loudspeaker had interrupted, "US Airways flight one-twenty-four for Pittsburgh is ready for boarding through Gate Sixteen. Passengers holding—"

"That's me." Kate started walking.

"Wait!" Molly grabbed her arm. "You're not coming back?"

"Well, not for nine years anyway." Kate smiled. "Don't forget, Molly. That's how long you're grounded."

On Monday, Kate had gone back to school. She figured Mr. Payne would drag her to his office two minutes after the first bell. Then he'd swat her with the paddle, demand a million dollars for his neck and a hundred for smoking, and finally suspend her for the rest of her life. Kate was scared, but after all she'd been through—put herself through—she knew she'd survive it.

What actually happened was a miracle. When she walked into Room 29, heart pounding and Noah clammed up, there was a substitute at Mr. Clouse's desk. Minh Duc was so excited she made the longest speech of her life:

"You should have been here Friday! Mr. Payne cleaned out his office, and he's gone! My dad complained to the superintendent about what he said, and the nurse was a witness, too. They call it administrative leave, but everybody says he's fired. Isn't it wonderful?"

"But where's Mr. Clouse?"

"Acting principal," Minh Duc said. "He's so *mad*! He

says now he'll never be able to hang up his snow shovel. Hey—" she added, "is that a new coat? Cute."

Later, Mr. Payne got himself in even more trouble because Mr. Mooney spotted him bowling, and his neck worked just fine; he wasn't even wearing the brace. Daddy said they should turn around and sue him right back. But Mom said no—when you live in a small town, you should try to get along.

At two o'clock, Kate's and Megan's moms appeared at the door of Room 29, holding plates of Valentine cookies and jugs of punch. "This must be the signal," said Ms. Springer, the new teacher.

Soon, with a lot of whispering and giggling, everyone was sorting envelopes and placing them in shoe boxes decorated the day before. "When you're finished," Ms. Springer said after a few minutes, "take two cookies and a glass of punch. Then you can go back to your desks to enjoy your cards."

"Hi, honey." Mom handed Kate a cookie.

"Thanks," said Kate. "It looks . . . hmm. You made 'em yourself, didn't you?" The cookie on Kate's napkin had once been heart-shaped, but some geologic episode had stretched, bent, and cracked it almost beyond recognition. The one Megan's mom presented Kate was perfect, right down to pink frosting and sprinkles.

I don't see how she got that job, Kate thought on her way back to her desk. Mom was now an assistant at the bakery by the courthouse. She baked scones all day.

When Kate flipped her shoe box over, she expected a few fluttering envelopes. Instead, there were so many they piled out, and some fell to the floor. Kate looked around. Were these the same kids who called her stuck-up? A liar? A snitch? The same kids who were ecstatic when she left the class in disgrace?

Yep, they were. Same kids. But maybe it was like the vulture that turned out to be a crow, and the gravedigger who turned out to be Mr. Douglas. They were only scary when they seemed strange. Now that Kate knew them better, they just seemed like regular kids: some snobby and some okay and some really nice.

Kate shuffled through the valentines. Emma's mom had come through with the chocolate. And here was one from Tiffany, who had only been suspended for a week after all. On the front was a picture of Minnie Mouse, with a little cigarette and a curling wisp of smoke inked in. "Ha-ha, just kidding—Tiff," said the note.

Very funny, Kate thought. Tiffany had come up to her at lunch one day and asked her about going back to California. "Is it true you took the bus to Pittsburgh by yourself? And even flew to L.A.?" Tiffany had never been out of Pennsylvania. Kate could see how what she'd done might look like a big adventure, but mostly it had been way scary and she didn't want to talk about it.

Kate saw Madison's name on a Daisy Duck card, and Ashley's on — what else? — a Snoopy card. Then there was a big envelope, and inside it a fancy card that folded down the middle, not the twenty-five-to-a-package kind everybody else gave. Kate's heart sank when she saw the signature: Ryan Kuhn. One good, hard push wasn't enough for some people.

Crunch-SCRA-A-A-PE, crunch-SCRA-A-A-PE, crunch-SCRA-A-A-PE, SNAP! Snowball was used to the sound of Mr. Douglas's shoveling, but that *snap* made her jump off Kate's bed with an irritated meow. It was a little after four Saturday morning. Kate got up, but before she made it to the window, she heard a roar that would wake the dead.

What the . . . !

Mom, Dad, and Danielle all came running. "It can't be legal," Mom said, "not at this hour."

"What is that horrible thing?" Danielle wanted to know.

"That horrible thing," Dad explained over the noise, "chews up the snow and spits it out. Same thing it does to honest manufacturers of snow shovels. It's called a snow-blower. And I don't care if we are neighbors, I'm calling the police."

He got about two steps before Mom called him back. "Coldwell?" She nodded toward the window. "You might want to reconsider."

Outside, Mr. Douglas had finished with his own sidewalk. Now he was clearing the Sommerses'.

In the morning, there was a line of broken shovels sunk in the snowbank by the Douglases' house — a picket fence of Flying Penguins. Daddy didn't think it was funny, but he didn't complain. He was too grateful that for once he didn't have to spend his Saturday shoveling.

After breakfast, Peter Douglas called and asked Kate to go skating. He would teach her. It was easy. But Kate was on her way next door to baby-sit Red-Suit. She'd be baby-sitting the rest of her life to pay off the airfare.

"What about tonight?"

"In the dark?"

"There's lights. Lotsa people skate at night."

"Peter, this isn't like a Valentine thing or something—"

"*No!* Absolutely not! No way!"

"Okay then."

"Okay."

So after dinner they walked into town, skates slung over their shoulders, just like kids in some cornball old movie, Kate thought. It was snowing lightly, but Kate was warm in her new parka. The pond, practically a lake by California standards, was surrounded by streetlamps, and there were red-and-white lanterns strung in the trees for Valentine's Day. The swirling snowflakes glinted pink.

Peter put his own skates on and waited patiently while Kate crossed lace after lace, tugging at the stiff leather.

"Now," he said when they got to the edge, "the thing about ice is—it's slippery." Kate's ankles felt wobbly, and she stepped carefully. Her blades had barely touched when they slid in opposite directions, and she had to grab Peter's hand.

"Now, uh, bend your knees," he said. "Keep loose. Keep your weight forward and, uh . . . *skate*."

Kate wondered if that was the entire lesson. But, keeping a firm grip on Peter's hand, she did as she was told. Push left, push right, push left . . . Much sooner than she expected, she caught Peter's rhythm and gained speed.

He looked back at her. "You learn fast."

"How do I stop?" She was a little breathless. "Like, if I'm gonna crash into somebody?"

"Pretty much the same as on in-line skates," Peter said. "Heel stop, T stop . . ."

Push left, push right . . . "How do *you* know how to stop on in-line skates?"

"From in-line skating. We play hockey on the tennis courts—see 'em?—in summer," he answered.

In-line skating? In Belletoona? Next he'd be telling her they surfed on the pond.

"Wanna race?" he asked her.

"I can't race!" But she took off after him anyway. They skated from the light at one end of the pond into the darkness at the other and back into the light. True, there was no rush of ocean, so sparkle of sunshine, no Talkin' Taco. But zooming along on the ice, snowflakes patting her face, Kate felt happy.

In bed that night, Kate got out the stationery Gramma had given her.

Dear Molly,

Happy Valentine's Day and thanks for the card. I think Bugs Bunny is cute, too.

I am sending you this ten-dollar bill so you can please send me my skates back.

Things are better. Dani pitched a homesick fit last week, but Daddy said they're going to name a new snow shovel after her: The Dancing-Ballerina-Snowflake Princess. Now she's okay, except she says she never wants to see another cup of hot chocolate.

Your mom told my mom Josh took that girl Mandy to the Valentine's dance. Too bad, chica. But I know how you feel.

Your Pennsylvania friend,

Kate